Contents

Acknowledgements

I would like to thank the following people for all the help and support they gave me in writing this book:

Julian Agyeman; Sue Meagher of Friends of the Earth; Christine Midgely of CEE; The publication team at WWF (who were invaluable in providing information on many habitat issues); Tessa Harrow of Souvenir Press for her patience despite one or two hitches; Shawn Askew for useful ideas and suggestions; the Vegetarian Society; the University of Arizona; Geof Cooper, Julie Gillet and many colleagues on the internet for information on Arctic pollution, groundwater pollution and recycling; Peter Capener, Centre for Sustainable Energy. Lastly, but certainly not least, thanks to my wife Swee Lean for all her patience and support.

1   Making a Start

These days, the word 'environment' always seems to be associated with environmental destruction, which can get pretty depressing. We don't hear much about the other side of the coin, environmental enhancement, but it offers a much more positive approach. Sure, you need to understand what has gone wrong in the past in order to work out how to put things right in the future—but even then you can look at things in a positive way. Progress and increased understanding are exciting stuff.

I want to concentrate on solutions. After all, the newspapers and nearly every other environmental book around has taken the gloomy approach to its limit. There are lots of good things going on. For the first time in our history we are beginning to come to terms with some of the fundamental problems facing the human race. That is pretty good news, even if progress often seems painfully slow.

My aim is to take a fresh and positive view of the world about us, looking at ways in which we can all help to make it a better place. The biggest mistake that people make about environmental problems is thinking that they are new and that we are individually to blame: they are not, and we are not. Our ability to change and manipulate the environment in a planned way is one of the fundamental things that makes human beings different from other animals. Of course animals do have an effect, but their behaviour owes more to instinct than to planning. Changing the world about us is a process that dates back to the first human being who cut down a tree to make room for grazing animals, perhaps even farther. And often changes have unexpected results. When the Romans grew grain on part of the northern Sahara, they didn't realise that their activity was likely to turn the area into a desert. But by no means all of our changes to the world about us have been bad—some have brought prosperity, health and education. It is just that, until recently, factors such as natural systems and the global environment were often left out of our calculations. The emphasis was on taming the wild, rather than living in harmony with it.

The exciting thing now is that we are beginning to understand the way our activities change the world, and to work out new ways to make the world a better, cleaner, healthier place to live, both for ourselves and the creatures around us. We are starting to understand how we can use resources more efficiently to reduce waste, and how we can harness natural forces to produce electrical power; to come up with imaginative solutions for the world's crises; to reclaim areas of desert made infertile by swirling sands for thousands of years. Yet what is even more exciting is that you can put yourself at the forefront of this new thinking and take a positive lead in the process. The challenge is to convert this knowledge into real change.

Your action makes a difference

The growing awareness of the environmental crisis has already done a lot to change things for the better. One of the most important environmental events in recent years was the United Nations Conference on Environment and Development held in Rio de Janeiro in June, 1992, when delegates from all over the world came together to debate a global agenda for change (see Chapter 9).

The following facts and figures show how practical measures to enhance the environment have made a difference in the United Kingdom. They might not be mind-blowing, but no one can deny that they show some progress:

- The amount of household waste being recycled rose from 2.4 per cent in 1983 to 5.9 per cent in 1993. Many local authorities are now aiming to recycle 20 per cent of their waste by the year 2000 (in line with UK government targets).
- In 1991, only 3 megawatts of wind power were installed in Britain. This increased to around 130 megawatts by the end of 1993.
- The number of students starting environmental science degrees increased from 244 in 1985 to 938 in 1992. Overall, many more students took degrees related to environmental issues. British universities are now aiming to introduce an environmental element across the curriculum.
- The number of bottle banks in the UK has risen from only 17 in 1977 to nearly 10,000 today.

❧ More than eight out of ten European businesses have appointed managers responsible for environmental measures in the last ten years.

All this is not to say that there are no problems. Indeed, our environment is under threat on a scale never before seen, and that threat is not going away. However, once we have acknowledged that a problem exists, the first question ought to be how can we improve the situation.

Quite often protecting the environment involves detective work, and the solution to a mystery is often more complex than it seems at first. For example, a number of years ago I was involved in an initiative to protect barn owls in the United Kingdom. These birds had become increasingly rare. At the time, much of the literature I read blamed this decline on the lack of suitable nesting sites, so our initiative started off by putting up nest boxes in suitable barns in the area around where I lived. But, after a survey of barns, it became obvious that there were already plenty of suitable nesting sites—in fact, owls have been recorded nesting between bales of hay in modern barns.

The reason for the decline of barn owls was likely to be more complicated. One rule of conservation is to look at the place of the species you wish to protect within the ecosystem. In the case of wild barn owls, the mainstay of their diet is the field vole, which lives in long-grass meadows. The owl often hunts by following the line of a hawthorn hedge, picking the voles from the long grass at the side of the field. Knowing this gives a good starting point for investigating the decline of the barn owl. A closer study of our area soon revealed a decrease in the area of grass meadows and hedgerows, with the spread of modern agricultural practices and intensive grazing. To put it simply, the barn owl's habitat had been largely destroyed.

But this was not a complete answer, as some suitable meadows did still exist. So I thought that one interesting tack would be to investigate the causes of death of barn owls, if such figures were available. I contacted three people: a specialist in barn owls who was then involved in the planned release of birds into the wild; an organisation called the Hawk Trust; and a wildlife shelter. The person concerned with the release of barn owls told me that one of the main considerations was to find sites away from busy roads. Because of the barn owls' method of hunting, birds were vulnerable to collision with motor vehicles. She also preferred organic farms where the risk of death due to pesticide poisoning would be reduced. The wildlife shelter told me that up to 80 per cent of the injured or dead owls they came across had been involved in collisions with motor vehicles. The Hawk Trust informed me further that the decline in the numbers of barn owls went back to the Victorian period, when birds were hunted as trophies and for use in

15

ornamentation. The reduced population had also suffered from a number of cold winters.

The barn owl (*Strix flammea*)

The story of the decline in barn owls was beginning to look increasingly complicated. It had no single cause, but rather a number of contributing factors: habitat loss, hedgerow loss, the use of modern pesticides, increasingly busy roads, cold winters and, lastly and perhaps least significantly, a lack of suitable nesting sites. So the right way to protect barn owls would be to protect those suitable habitats that exist already, and to encourage farmers to leave meadows undisturbed.

This is a theme I shall be coming back to in this book. The answers aren't always easy; there is rarely a single cause for environmental degradation. But understanding the problems, and therefore finding the solutions, is all about making connections between different areas of knowledge. What made me excited was discovering that those people involved in barn owl conservation were already working with farmers to produce suitable habitats for the re-establishment of the species. In addition, heightened awareness has made nature conservation an international issue, so everyone was taking it more seriously.

Politicians have become increasingly willing to listen to the opinion of conservationists and take action on a national scale. Sometimes this action is tempered with environmental blunders, but at least it represents progress. When you are dealing with practical conservation, politics can seem very distant—but that does not lessen the importance of political action. At the end of the day, if you want to make something happen nationally, the best way is to get involved in a campaign. Even if the campaign doesn't succeed in meeting all of its goals, at least people are made more aware of what can be done.

There is a number of simple practical things that you can do to protect and improve the environment, and many will be discussed later in this book. As far as wildlife is concerned, measures such as starting a nature garden can help. If you are willing to do the detective work necessary to find out the particular niche in the ecosystem of a rare species of plant or animal in your local area, then you can create conditions conducive to that particular species. This is more difficult in some cases than others—with predators of any kind, for instance, the problem is one of protecting a large enough area. This is because of the way energy moves in food chains.

Every time energy moves along a food chain some of it is lost. For example, when a cow eats grass some of the energy in the grass is lost because the cow needs quite a lot of it just to keep warm, breathe and move around. This means that there is less food energy for any carnivores eating the cows. The overall effect is that there are likely to be fewer carnivores than herbivores and they will each, therefore, have a larger hunting area than the grazing area of the herbivores they consume. This need for a large hunting territory is one reason why, worldwide, there are so many large predators on the list of endangered species.

The rest of this chapter will explore some of the attitudes to the world about us. This fascinating area lies at the heart of the current environmental debate. And since our attitudes are the basis of nearly everything we do, it is the right place to start. A wide range of views exists about the role of human beings in the natural world, and examining them should help you to decide your own views before we start to explore deeper.

Human attitudes to nature

In the past human beings have regarded the natural world as a resource to be exploited. Animals and peoples living in natural systems have often been hunted to the point of extinction, or land has been cleared, which has had an even more devastating effect. These attitudes and actions, more than anything, led to the destruction of many natural systems.

Many religions and systems of moral belief take a view on the relationship between human beings and the natural world. Buddhists see the wild creatures of the earth as an important and integral part of the human world, and therefore adopt a policy of not causing harm to other species. Christianity, on the other hand, sees humans as fundamentally different from and superior to other animals, giving them a role as stewards and guardians of the natural world. But no system of moral belief would condone the wholesale destruction of our natural world. So how did we arrive at the situation we are in today?

I think that the answer is that, in the past, the moral implications of destroying natural systems were rarely considered. But even at the beginning of this century there were different views on our relationship with the environment, as shown by this extract from *Wayside and Woodland Ferns* by Edward Step, published in 1908:

> It must be admitted with sorrow that ferns are far less plentiful in our land to-day than they were in the memory of many still living. The senseless cupidity that compels people to possess themselves of anything they know to be rare without considering whether they can make any use of it, has led to the needless destruction of a number of species. In the vicinity of some of our larger towns and cities, where ferns were formerly abundant, not one is now to be found. The hawker, the exchange club botanist, and the town amateur gardener have been largely responsible for this condition of things, and now we have the additional menace of nature-study classes, which might be more fitly named nature-suppression classes, for the main outcome of their efforts is the destruction of many thousands of specimens.

Due to a growing awareness of the changes brought about by human beings, our attitudes to nature have begun to change. It is now widely recognised that the way we view our relationship with other species is crucial to shaping our view of the environment. The preservation of habitats is now seen as being at the heart of conservation work.

Why not discuss attitudes to the natural world with your friends and family? Find out what sort of views people hold these days. If you are religious you might like to find out more about your religion's view. Some beliefs have long seen certain animals as having religious significance. The Incas, for example, saw the llama as sacred. Many religions see elephants as sacred.

The Story of Ganesh

Ganesh is a popular Hindu god. He has the head of an elephant and the body of a man. He brings good fortune, and his name can be called in prayers to bring good fortune to new enterprises or new books. Ganesh is the son of Siva, who is said to have cut off the boy's head in a fit of anger. He was then sorry for what he had done and replaced it with the head of the nearest animal, which happened to be an elephant.

GANESH

Ancient Hindu books frequently refer to elephants; one, *Gajasastra*, is all about them. Many Hindu temples in India keep elephants for ceremonial purposes. In Sri Lanka, a giant elephant carries a tooth, supposed to be one of Buddha's, during the festival of Esala Perahera.

AIMING FOR SUSTAINABILITY

How we go about redefining our relationship with the world about us has led to widespread debate. Over the years environmentalists have tried to come up with hypotheses and models to pin down some of their ideas. Perhaps the best known of these is the Gaia hypothesis put forward by Dr

James Lovelock, which sees the world as a self-sustaining unit. Much recent debate has focused on how we can develop a type of society that is ecologically sustainable.

As a result of these debates, the environmental vocabulary has burgeoned—in terms of generating jargon, some of the environmental reports that come out are only rivalled by specialist computer manuals. But the concepts that many of these words hide are often really very simple. There have been whole books written to try to define the term 'sustainable development', for example, and many of them are important works. But what most people want is a word they can get hold of. So let's go for it. Sustainability just means creating a system that allows us to hand something on to our children which is worth at least as much in environmental terms as the one we received from our parents. It is, if you like, creating a system of human activity that enhances and maintains rather than destroys the planet. Within the environmental movement there exists a whole range of views on how we go about achieving sustainability. These have sometimes been described in terms of shades of green, with dark green usually representing those who think that very deep fundamental change is necessary to bring about sustainability and light green being used to describe those who feel that our current system can accommodate environmental concerns with relatively little change.

Whichever view you take, environmentalism has a strong political element. These days, nearly every political party has a green lobby. There are also green parties throughout the world. Perhaps the most successful is the German green party, which has captured up to 10 per cent of the popular vote. It is worth discussing the political implications of environmentalism with your friends and making up your own mind.

Environment and science

Another area to discuss is the relationship between environmentalism and science. Some people have accused environmentalists of being anti-science, though I find that a little odd, particularly bearing in mind the amount of environmental research undertaken by science graduates. But the way we use science and technology has given rise to much debate, because our use of science reflects our attitudes to the environment. Badly used science and technology can destroy whole ecosystems alarmingly quickly. But science can also be a powerful tool for good.

Why not discuss the relationship between science and nature with your friends and teachers, and examine a few areas of conflict? In my view, to make this world sustainable we will need all of our science and know-how—

maybe even a little more. But making society sustainable will require enormous social change, and that will certainly not happen overnight. This is particularly the case if you bear in mind the earth's soaring population.

Population growth

Since the time of the economist Thomas Malthus, who in the eighteenth century argued that nature has its own ways of limiting populations, people have speculated that an ever-increasing population will eventually lead to famine on a massive scale. This has not yet proved true. The fact is that the earth can feed the present human population, and theoretically perhaps far more. But what are still of serious concern are the triple threats of runaway population growth, growing poverty and environmental degradation. These pressures make widespread famine in the so-called developing world ever more likely. In addition, the ever-increasing demand for energy and natural resources continues to put environments throughout the world under increasing pressure. The average US citizen consumes 50 times more than the average Kenyan citizen. If everyone lived the rich life style of many of those in the northern hemisphere, our planet simply could not cope. On the other hand, who would say that anyone should have a life style worse than we enjoy ourselves?

Controlling population growth is something that must be handled by governments and at an international level, through family-planning programmes and through encouraging adequate systems of education and social support. Encouraging a more sustainable life style is something that everyone can be involved in, and the onus is on the rich nations to make better use of the resources they have at their disposal. But it is important to keep population control on the agenda in developed as well as less-developed countries.

If you are concerned about the runaway growth of the Earth's population, you should get in touch with one of the organisations campaigning on this issue, such as The WorldWatch Institute in the US and Population Concern in the UK. Their addresses are at the back of the book. It is also worth having a look at some of the material published by WorldWatch which examines the implications for feeding the world in the next century.

MYTH-BUSTERS

To dispel some of the common environmental myths and over-simplifications, I have included a myth-busters section in some chapters. For even-handedness, some have been included from both sides of the environmental debate—even environmentalists get things wrong occasionally.

Africa

There are so many myths about Africa that it is a good idea to bust several at the same time. For a start it is far less densely populated than many people realise, with only 16 people per square kilometre (40 people per square mile), compared with 200 or 300 in much of the developed world. Around half of the poor people in Africa live in the most environmentally vulnerable areas, and it is often pressure on these marginal lands that gives rise to famine. Developing sustainable strategies for agriculture in such areas is a top priority.

- Between 1979 and 1989, Africa's share of world trade fell from 3.8 per cent to 1 per cent.
- In sub-Saharan Africa, one-fifth of government spending goes in debt repayments, which is more than is spent on health and education combined.
- Africa has more than 20 per cent of the world's growing land but only 9 per cent of its people.
- A movement of 50,000 women in Kenya planted some 10 million trees.
- In Africa most working women are farmers; more women than men are farmers, and women grow 90 per cent of the food.

THE POVERTY TRAP: RICH AND POOR

In many countries a growing population is combined with extreme poverty, putting immense pressure on people and land alike. Poor people are more likely to have large families, which in turn increases pressure on the environment. This leads to a spiral of malnutrition, famine and environmental degradation. Poverty is undoubtedly one of the greatest threats to the environment today. Poverty leads to problems such as overgrazing on some of the world's most marginal lands, and exacerbates the effects of droughts and other natural disasters.

Poor people who are barely able to eke out a living can hardly be blamed for cutting down trees or overgrazing lands. The solutions to global poverty are not simple or straightforward, but there are a few useful starting points. Better trade deals for developing nations would help, since currently around $40,000 million moves from south to north every year. Reducing debt in the developing world would also help give poor nations a better chance. Many

22

Repair in the developing world, waste in the developed world. This is a pattern that is found all too often.

of the loans that now so burden developing nations were made at a time when commodity prices were high and there was every reason for governments to believe that they could accelerate development by borrowing. Since then many commodity prices have tumbled, and whole nations have been left in a hopeless position. In some cases the original sums have been paid off several times over, but the debt remains due to payment of interest.

Increased resources alone will not provide a complete solution, but they would help to alleviate some of the disparity that currently exists. Too often, money flowing into countries with tyrannical, undemocratic regimes benefits only a tiny proportion of the population and does nothing to protect the environment. Even in democratic countries, funds may be used for projects that threaten to destroy natural habitats. Ultimately a type of development has to be encouraged which allows countries to live sustainably, both economically and environmentally. In order to achieve this, a global change of attitude is needed, with aid and funds being given to those projects most likely to bring environmental as well as economic benefit, together with measures to give developing countries a fairer deal.

Encouraging sustainable development requires governments or agencies to work with local people on small-scale projects, such as teaching farmers simple techniques to avoid desertification, or helping to provide clean water or biofuel for villages. Aid for projects that enhance local environments is usually far better than aid for grand schemes such as building huge new power stations or roads, many of which are environmentally damaging.

Even schemes aimed at helping improve the environment have backfired because local people were not involved. Perhaps the best-known example of this is reforestation through the planting of fast-growing species of tree such as eucalyptus in India and elsewhere. In some cases, trees were quickly removed for firewood or uprooted in protest, since they often replaced grazing land. The benefit to poor people has often been negligible. Planting schemes involving the local population have a far better record of success: in India, the Chipko movement is the most famous example of grass-roots initiatives aimed at protecting forests.

Taking action

If you wish to become involved in the fight to give developing nations a better deal, I would advise you to work with, or raise funds for, one of the many voluntary organisations working in the developing world. Many of the schemes operated by these agencies are excellent and genuinely help to relieve poverty and encourage sustainable development.

ENVIRONMENTAL RIGHTS

These days most people consider themselves to be entitled to basic health care and education. But the link between the quality of the environment and the quality of life is often neglected. By this I do not mean environmental health, but rather issues such as pollution levels and access to natural resources. Improving the environment leads to improvements in the quality of life. What we should be working towards is the idea that we all have a right to live in an unpolluted environment in the same way as we have a right to health care and education. Today most people object to breathing in someone else's cigarette smoke, but far fewer people seem to object to breathing in someone else's car exhaust fumes, even though pollutants from cars have now been shown to aggravate childhood asthma and breathing difficulties. In Tokyo it is even possible to purchase small cans of oxygen in order to alleviate the symptoms caused by exposure to the city's chronic exhaust fumes.

Among disadvantaged groups such as ethnic minorities, basic environmental protection often takes a low priority. In the United States, a report by the Environmental Protection Agency in 1992 showed that ethnic minorities suffer disproportionate exposure to dust, soot, carbon monoxide, ozone, sulphur, sulphur dioxide, lead, and emissions from hazardous waste dumps. Many local protests have arisen as a result of this environmental disparity, leading to the development of a national environmental justice movement. So awareness of these issues among disadvantaged groups can help to bring about change.

Case study—the Navajo

The Navajo reservation is located on the New Mexico–Arizona border in the southern USA. A serious pollution incident occurred in 1979, when 425 million litres (94 million gallons) of radioactive waste were released into the Puerco River due to an accident at the United Nuclear Corporation's Church Rock Mill near Gallup, New Mexico.

The river, which winds through the reservation and the communities of Manuelito and Lupton, remains polluted to this day. As a result, the 10,000 Navajos who live along the Puerco must use shallow wells and springs to draw water for their livestock and personal needs. At the time the spill was neither publicised nor taken seriously by the tribe. But as a result there was a dramatic rise in animal deformities and cancer-related deaths among tribe members living along the river. Voluntary agencies working in the area have now helped the tribe secure unpolluted sources of water.

Legislation in the late 1980s gave native Americans the authority to set their own standards and regulations, and many tribes are now involved in taking environmental decisions on reservations. Tribes such as the Umatilla in Oregon, the Sioux in South Dakota, the Kaibab-Paiute in Arizona, the Kaw in Oklahoma and the Choctaw in Mississippi have rejected proposals to place toxic landfill sites on their reservations. The tribes, working together with county planning boards and state and federal agencies, have been able to influence environmental decisions. In many cases, this has helped them preserve the environment in which they live. But there are also examples which show that tribes remain easy targets for exploitation (see Chapter 7).

ACTIVITIES

Everyone can help in protecting the environment. The role of the individual should never be underestimated: many of the initiatives that have benefited the environment have originated as a result of individual concern. For example, in many countries the increase in the number of cars fitted with catalytic converters directly parallels the rise in public concern. What is more, when the public become aware of an issue, politicians are rarely far behind. As a result of consumer pressure many manufacturers have begun to market greener products. In fact, so many products have been produced that claim to be 'green' that the public have often ended up quite bewildered. The issues surrounding green consumerism are dealt with in Chapter 8.

Here are a few ways that you can become involved in protecting the environment:

Recycling

The easiest items to recycle on a local scale are bottles, cans and paper. However, if you have a garden one of the first things you should consider is building a compost heap. In the developed world around a quarter of all waste is organic waste, and much of this can be composted. Furthermore, organic waste contributes significantly to the build-up of methane in landfill sites. The presence of organic waste in household waste also makes sorting for recycling more difficult. Some local authorities have developed innovative schemes to remove organic waste from rubbish and compost it on municipal compost heaps. Often these schemes involve issuing householders with separate bins for garden and other organic waste. If this has not yet happened in your area you don't have to wait—why not take action in your own back yard. Developing your own compost heap is easy and fun (see Chapter 3).

Energy use

Many simple measures can help to conserve energy. Switching off unused electrical items is only one way of reducing energy consumption. Perhaps the best overall method of saving energy is home insulation or, in the case of countries with hot climates, low-energy methods of keeping buildings cool. If your house is uninsulated, ask your parents to insulate it.

It may surprise you to learn that reuse and recycling also help to reduce energy consumption. The reason for this is that products require energy for their manufacture, and goods made from recycled materials require less energy in their production. In the case of aluminium cans, the reduction is around 90 per cent.

Building a wildlife area

Many groups of young people have become involved in developing wildlife areas, either on land near their school or on disused ground. The best way to become involved in this type of initiative is to join a local group. In Britain, the organisation BTCV (British Trust for Conservation Volunteers) organises many activities for young people in developing and improving wildlife areas.

Eco-gardening

If you enjoy gardening, you may be interested in setting up an organic garden. As more gardeners become involved in the production of fruit and vegetables through organic methods, so expertise and resources increase.

PROJECTS

Make an environmental map of your area

A good way to find out a little more about your local area is to draw a map to include the main environmental features. You might include, for example, such things as areas of woodland, long grass, mountain terrain, or even areas of unkempt garden and scrubland, which are surprisingly good for nature conservation. If you live near an unusual habitat such as mud flats, peatlands or semi-arid or arid lands, don't forget to include these too. But you should not only include features that enhance the environment: try to identify some of the main causes of pollution and environmental degradation in your area. While this might be quite easy if you live near a busy main road or a smoky factory, in some areas identifying environmental hazards can be far more difficult. Where I live, for example, the most obvious local environmental hazard is an enormous gravel pit which takes a little finding if you don't know where it is.

Once you have drawn your environmental map you can go on to make a rough plan of ways in which your local environment could be improved. You may include some ideas like traffic-calming measures or planting trees. You could even make a model of your area to plan possible improvements. One interesting way to draw your maps is by using a computer package. Once

27

you have your map, you can enter statistics from survey work covered in other parts of this book.

Environmental-mapping is a fascinating subject. Maps can be used to discover how a particular environment has changed over a period of time, or simply to portray the state of a particular environment. With the aid of computers it is possible to overlay one map on top of another and discover possible areas of correlation between environmental factors. For example, it would be possible visually to compare the number of cases of childhood asthma with the recorded level of air pollution. One method of doing this is through what is known as a GIS, or geographic information system, package.

The environmental eyesore competition

Organise a competition among your friends to find out who can find the biggest environmental eyesore in your local area. First, draw up and agree on a list of environmental criteria for use in making judgements. Survey a different part of the area each, looking at all the eyesores you can find. Then go round together and jointly judge which is the worst area. Once you have done this try to work out how the place you have picked as the town's worst environmental eyesore could be improved. Begin by making a list of all the things about your local eyesore that make it ugly or environmentally unsound.

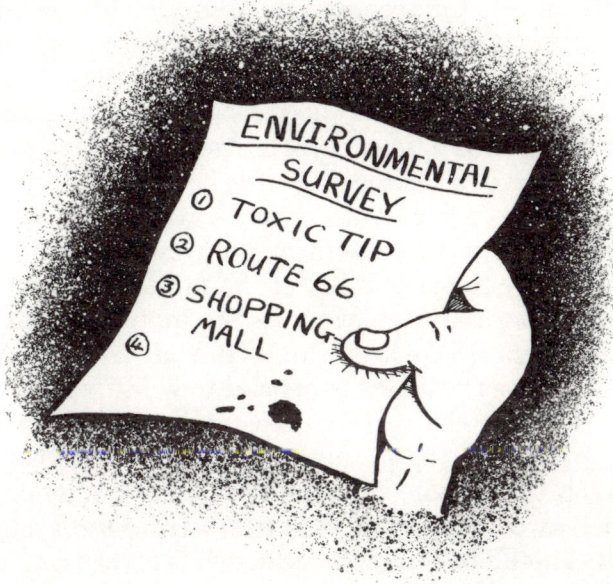

Once you have identified the problems, see if you can begin to work out the solutions. Some of these might be remarkably simple. For example, you might decide that the area you have identified could be considerably improved by the planting of a few strategically placed trees. You can even take this exercise further. For instance, you could draw up improved rough plans of the area and then contact your local council or the company concerned to present your plans and ask if they intend doing anything to improve the site. You can point out that it is very difficult for people to have positive attitudes to the environment if they themselves live in a run-down and ugly area. Local politicians will often give a group putting ideas forward a sympathetic hearing. From their point of view, removing obvious eyesores equates to votes. If you want to undertake this type of lobbying activity, get together with a group of friends (see Chapter 9). If you are at school or

29

college, it would be a good idea to involve an interested teacher or lecturer in your activity.

Environmental beauty spot competition

Once you have found the worst eyesore in your area, try to find what you consider the best place environmentally. You might decide on a place that is good for wildlife or one that represents environmental good practice. Use your list of environmental criteria, and survey an area each. Again, look at the reasons why you chose the place you did. You might, for example, choose an area of woodland or a particularly good recycling centre. Ask some critical questions about the area you have chosen. Are there ways in which it could be made more attractive to visitors? Or if it is a facility, are there ways in which it could be made easier to use or more attractive? You might decide that even the area you have chosen for your environmental beauty spot could be improved. Try to make a list of the attributes that make an area visually attractive. Are they the same as the qualities that make a place environmentally beneficial? Discuss this with your friends. You might find, for example, that an area which is beneficial to wildlife is not neat and tidy in the traditional sense. Conversely, you might decide that a pedestrian precinct is more attractive than a highway jammed with cars.

You can develop this theme even further with a role-play of a council meeting in which two groups put views forward. One group feels that a particular facility should be removed because it is an eyesore, and the second group feels that the facility should be kept because it is environmentally beneficial. Are you able to reach a compromise?

Suggest an environment week

Why not get your school or college to run an environment week? Even though these often end up scheduled for the end of the academic year, they provide a useful focus for the whole school to get involved in environmental initiatives. It is best to concentrate on just one environmental issue; otherwise you end up with too much to cover in one week. You may decide to hold an energy week, for example. You can find some ideas of the type of activities you might suggest in Chapter 7.

2 Recycling

Recycling is a good, practical way to protect the environment. Nearly every form of recycling saves energy and reduces the need to exploit precious resources. But recycling is by no means a straightforward subject. Our society is in part based on the idea of ever-increasing consumption, which in turn means more and more waste, and, in environmental terms, building things to last is better than constantly recycling material. In order to tackle some of the world's environmental problems, we need to re-evaluate the way we use materials, and the best way of helping to do this is by becoming involved in one of the many environmental campaigns aimed at promoting the sustainable use of resources. Despite this note of caution, recycling is still good practice, and there are very few materials that cannot be recycled in one way or another.

In order to fully understand the process of recycling, it is necessary to make a distinction between recycling and reuse. Recycling involves the reprocessing, in one way or another, of materials that have already been used. The scrap-metal industry, for example, recycles cars and metals to make new items. This obviously reduces the need to exploit new areas for the extraction of iron ore. Reuse, in contrast, involves using an item again directly, without reprocessing. Containers of different descriptions are obvious candidates for reuse. Glass bottles, for example, can be reused as many as 20 times before they require recycling.

The four Rs provide a pretty good way to order your priorities: refuse, reuse, repair, recycle.

1 *Refuse*

Refuse to buy goods with unneeded packaging. Even more importantly before you buy something, ask yourself whether or not you really need it.

2 *Reuse*

Many items can be reused easily. Milk bottles, for example, can be refilled from 20–40 times. Envelopes and scrap paper are also candidates for reuse.

3 *Repair*

Many items that are thrown away could be repaired. Once it was far easier to get items repaired than it is today, which perhaps reflects the increasingly 'throw away' nature of our consumption. In many developing countries repair of items such as umbrellas, cases, shoes and so on is still widespread.

4 *Recycle*

Find out about local recycling facilities. Most councils run local recycling depots, some even organise doorstep collection, while others organise collections from local businesses and schools.

The highest priority is to reduce consumption, so if you consider goods to be overpackaged, write to the manufacturers and ask if they have thought about reducing costs by removing superfluous packaging. Point out that doing so may give them an environmental edge over their competitors. Some goods such as electrical products, of course, do require packaging to avoid damage in transit. But in such cases manufacturers can consider using recycled materials in their packaging, and a lot of them are very amenable to this idea, since by using materials such as shredded paper they can help reduce costs.

During the recycling boom in the late 1980s, stories were going around about people consuming more simply in order to generate material for recycling. You may laugh, but it is not always easy to avoid environmental boo-boos. For example, if you are only recycling a small amount of material, the energy used to get to the local recycling point might be greater than the energy saved by recycling the material in the first place. That is one reason why doorstep collections of recyclable goods are better than 'bring' systems; they also ensure that more material is recycled.

Bear in mind that recycling should be a last resort, and that it is not cost-effective to recycle some items. Many products which are a mixture of different materials are very difficult to reprocess. At the end of the day, whatever we do will produce some waste. If your overall aim is to minimise the amount of waste you create, then you are probably not going far wrong environmentally.

33

The combined effect of awareness-raising and recycling does make a difference. In the London borough of Westminster, there has been a decrease of more than 10 per cent in the tonnage of waste collected for landfill over the last three years. The combined effect of the borough's recycling scheme and heightened awareness has undoubtedly contributed to this reduction.

Waste throughout the world

Many developing countries produce far less waste than the richer Western nations. This not only reflects greater affluence, and therefore greater consumption, but also different attitudes to resources. The richer the country, the more waste its people tend to produce. The following table compares the amount of rubbish produced, per person per day, in various parts of the world.

City	Country	Rubbish produced (kg/person/day
New York	USA	1.8 (3lb 12oz)
Hamburg	Germany	0.85 (1lb 12oz)
Rome	Italy	0.69 (1lb 7oz)
Hong Kong	Hong Kong	0.85 (1lb 12oz)
Kano	Nigeria	0.46 (1lb)
Medellin	Colombia	0.54 (1lb 3oz)
Jakarta	Indonesia	0.60 (1lb 4oz)
London	United Kingdom	0.77 (1lb 10oz)

It is not only the amount of rubbish produced that varies from country to country; what is in the rubbish also differs. The percentage of recyclable goods found in waste in developed countries tends to be far higher than the amount found in developing countries.

City	Country	Percentage of paper, metal, glass, plastic	Percentage of organic waste	Percentage other
London	United Kingdom	55	28	17
Kano	Nigeria	28	43	29
Medellin	Colombia	30	56	14
Jakarta	Indonesia	10	50	40

Not only do the developed countries produce more waste, they also produce more recyclable waste.

Recycling in the developing world

Often in developing countries much less waste is produced because people are much better at reusing or recycling what they have than we are. Part of the reason for this is the lower level of disposable incomes, but also, in countries where materials are scarce, it is understood that protecting them is vital. For those people who live in North America or Europe, the seemingly endless flow of resources can make it difficult to keep things in perspective.

Shanghai

Some of the most interesting examples of recycling in action come from China. Shanghai, with a population of around 12 million people, produces about 13 million tonnes of solid waste each year. The city's reprocessing and recycling project raises enough money to cover the costs of its collection

35

and disposal, and to employ 29,000 people. Organic waste taken is converted into biogas in more than 1,000 village plants, which supply 60,000 households; it is also used to make fertiliser. Reclaimed products are sold in shops throughout the city. In all, more than 1,000 types of materials are reprocessed including ferrous and non-ferrous metals, rubber, plastics, paper, rags, animal bones and waste oil.

Liuminying village

The development of village biogas facilities has had many knock-on effects which might not be apparent at first. In Liuminying village near Beijing, the installation of biogas proved beneficial to villagers by providing a cleaner and healthier method of cooking. It also helped reduce the risk of infection from gastric diseases and roundworm by providing a safe method of sewage treatment for people and animals alike. What is more, the dregs from biogas tanks can be used as fertiliser on fields. Since the active bacteria in the tanks have killed a high proportion of harmful pathogens—substances that spread disease—the resulting compost is far safer to use than raw animal dung. This type of methane generator provides a cheap and useful way for developing countries to produce fuel for cooking while helping to improve public health. Since the installation of the biogas plant, the village has now developed a mixed system of agriculture, which uses the methane dregs as fertiliser. As a result the village has increased crop yields, while many visitors have been attracted to the area to see what is often described as a model eco-village.

In the richer Western nations it is possible to develop biogas on a much grander scale, one of the most common sources being old landfill sites. The gas from these has variously been used to produce electricity, heat swimming pools and heat municipal buildings. While this does not provide an excuse for the landfilling of waste, it does serve as a useful way of utilising existing resources.

MATERIALS FOR RECYCLING

Paper

In most homes and colleges a lot of high-quality paper is simply thrown away. Exercise books, writing, photocopy and computer paper are all made of paper that ought to be recycled.

An important way to help with the efforts to recycle more paper is to purchase goods made from recycled pulp. These days it is quite easy to

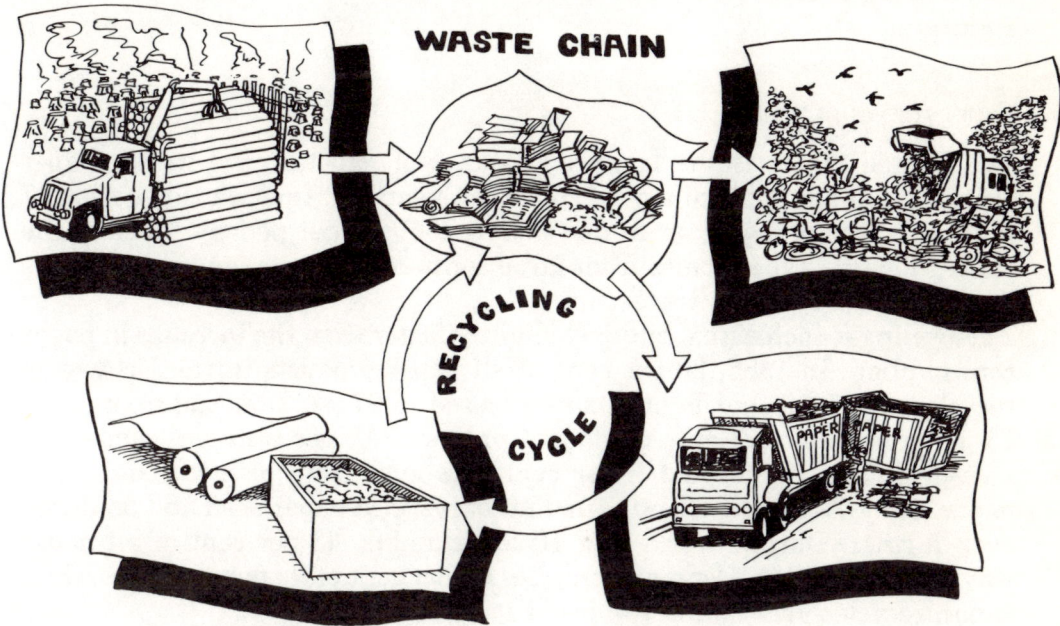

WASTE CHAIN

RECYCLING CYCLE

purchase recycled exercise books and note pads, and recycled paper can be used for photocopying and writing letters, as well as being made into toilet rolls, tissues, blotting paper and card. Two factors which have prevented the increased use of recycled paper have been its higher price and lower quality. Because less energy is needed for milling paper from recycled pulp, one might suppose that the resulting products would be cheaper than goods made from virgin pulp. Although this is not always so, it is just a case of supply and demand—as the quantity of paper produced from recycled pulp increases, so the cost will come down. Some recycled products such as tissues and toilet rolls are already cheaper than their equivalents. The quality issue is a little more tricky, since fibres of recycled paper are not as strong as those found in non-recycled paper. Nevertheless, it is possible to produce paper of a reasonably high quality, certainly more than adequate for everyday use, and where a higher quality is necessary, it is possible to produce a paper made from a mixture of recycled and non-recycled pulp.

I have used recycled paper for years, and I have never found it lacking in terms of durability. Nor have I found that it sticks on photocopiers or printers as some people claim. Photocopiers sometimes need resetting to cope with a different thickness of paper, but this is something that the

37

service technician should be able to sort out. When you are purchasing recycled paper look for the unbleached variety: chlorine bleaching is highly polluting.

Paper recycling in the USA

The United States is the largest consumer of paper in the world. Paper consumption has doubled since 1965. Each year the Americans use over 67 million tonnes of paper, or around 300 kg (660 lb) per person. Much of the timber for this paper comes from large coniferous forests, and most of this paper ends up in landfill sites.

Recycling is increasing, but only slightly faster than the increase in paper consumption. In 1985, 20 per cent of all paper products in the USA were recycled. By 1989 that figure had increased to 27 per cent; approximately 75 per cent was made into cardboard products, 17 per cent was made into newsprint and tissue, and 8 per cent was made into printing and office paper. The US can increase the amount of recycled paper used and produced even further. During World War II, for example, 43 per cent of all paper was recycled. Today, Denmark recycles 60 per cent of its paper waste, while Japan recycles over half of the paper it uses.

MYTH-BUSTERS

Save a tree

Recycling paper is excellent practice. It saves energy, reduces the pressure on resources, and helps relieve pressure on habitats. But, unfortunately for the slogan-makers, there is not necessarily a direct equation between recycling paper and saving trees. The 'save a tree' slogan is appealing, but it has sometimes been picked up by the forestry lobby as being inaccurate: paper is often made from forest thinnings and offcuts, not from mature trees which are used for timber. Even so, some forest plantations are grown with the primary purpose of producing pulp for paper production. In addition, some trees are grown on areas with a higher conservation value than forest plantation, such as the flow-lands in Scotland. Not all forests are good for conservation—forest monocultures of non-native species have a lower conservation value than forests containing native tree species (see Chapter 3). So on some occasions conservationists may be trying to stop trees being planted rather than saving them.

Making recycled paper is polluting

Before paper can be recycled the ink must be removed through a process known as de-inking. Although the de-inking can be polluting, making recycled paper is overall far less polluting than making paper from virgin pulp, particularly with unbleached recycled paper.

Glass

Most glass used for producing items such as bottles currently finds its way into landfill sites—and that's a lot of glass. The United Kingdom, for example, with a population of around 60 million, uses 6 billion glass bottles and jars every year, one every day in every household. Reusing bottles is the best way to recycle them—a milk-bottle starts paying for itself after 25 refills. Otherwise, making new glass from smashed old bottles, called cullet, saves a lot of energy: 135 litres (30 gallons) of oil are saved for every tonne of glass recycled. Quarrying sand and limestone for new glass is also damaging for the environment.

Textiles

Old clothes can be used for lots of things. They can be worn by other people, or pulled apart and respun to make new clothes, furniture stuffing, blankets and roofing felt.

Plastics

Plastics are difficult materials to recycle for a number of reasons. One of the biggest problems is that plastic products often use more than one type of plastic, and separating them is difficult and not cost-effective. Some products such as fence posts can be manufactured from mixed plastics, but the applications are limited.

At the manufacturing level, relatively little scrap reaches the waste stream because it is reprocessed. Around 75 per cent of thermoplastic and 22 per cent of commercial scrap is recovered. However, less than 1 per cent of domestic plastic ends up being recycled. The average rate of recovery for all plastics in Europe as a whole is less than 10 per cent.

Some manufacturers have begun to produce bottles from easily recyclable plastics. Often plastic items are marked if they are recyclable. Nevertheless, partly because of the lack of plastic recycling schemes, most of these bottles end up in landfill sites. If you intend recycling plastics, they should be separated into different categories according to which polymer they are made from: PET, PVC and HDPE are the most commonly recycled plastics.

- ❦ PET (polythene terephthalate) is a common flexible plastic. Used in fizzy-drinks bottles, for example.
- ❦ PVC (polyvinylchloride) is one of the most common types of plastic. Often used for drinks bottles, household goods such as shampoos, and film wrappings.
- ❦ HDPE (high density polyethylene) is often used in large milk containers and bottles for household cleaners.
- ❦ OTHERS Polystyrene, polypropylene and other types of plastics are also commonly used in food tubs, etc. Most of these plastics are not currently recycled, although the technology to do this does exist.

Organic matter

Organic matter is the biggest item in municipal waste, making up around a quarter of the total in most developed countries. If this type of waste was collected separately, it could be composted and sold to farmers and gardeners as an organic fertiliser and soil conditioner. At present only a small quantity of organic waste is treated in this way, but it would make sense for the majority of organic waste to be treated using municipal composting and anaerobic digestion. Some local authorities have begun looking at ways in which this can happen.

For local authorities aiming to increase the amount of recycled waste, organic composting can provide an excellent way forward because, once organic waste is removed, the separation of other items within the waste stream becomes more feasible. Organic matter is one of the main components of waste responsible for producing methane gas in landfill sites. By digesting the organic component, it is possible to make biogas for local use, as we have already seen in Shanghai. Using organic matter for composting also has the benefit of reducing the reliance of the horticulture industry on composts extracted from natural sources, such as garden peat taken from peat bogs in Finland, Ireland and the United Kingdom. The wholesale extraction of peat has led to the destruction of rare wildlife habitats, including some internationally important sites. Open heathlands of the type used for peat extraction provide nesting grounds for many species of birds, and also contain their own unique flora and fauna.

If your local authority does not currently operate a municipal composting scheme it is worth writing to them and suggesting that at least they should look into it. Schools and colleges can compost organic waste from their

canteens too, although very few do so at present. If you go to school or
college you could suggest that the authorities might consider this as a part
of an overall package aimed at improving their environmental performance.

Recycling rates in Europe and North America

Country	Glass	Aluminium Cans	Steel Cans
France	34%	negligible	24%
Italy	40%	29%	Not available
Netherlands	53%	negligible	45%
Norway	6%	80%	Not available
Sweden	22%	82%	Not available
Switzerland	55%	26%	Not available
UK	20%	10%	10%
USA	34%	60%	20%
West Germany	39%	negligible	45%

Precycle before you recycle

Precycling is a name used to refer to reducing waste by reuse, reduction
and repair. The University of Arizona in the USA has produced a fact sheet
listing the following precycling action points. Though some mainly apply to
the USA, I consider them as good as any I have seen:

- Buy products in glass containers. Wash them out when empty. Then, either reuse the container for bulk goods bought at the supermarket, for leftovers (instead of plastic wrap or foil), or recycle the glass after removing the lid.
- Buy in bulk and transfer the bulk goods to your empty glass containers. Better yet, bring your glass containers to the shop and fill directly with bulk goods. Some goods that come in bulk are peanut butter, rice, baking supplies, cereals, spices and teas, as well as body-care products such as soap, shampoo and lotion.
- Take reusable bags to the stores you shop at (not just the grocer but all kinds of stores). If you do use paper bags, you sometimes receive a discount for taking them back to be used for your next purchase.
- Take your favourite mug or a thermos to the coffee shop. You will save paper, and many coffee shops offer discounted prices when you bring your own mug or thermos.
- Repair broken items and use durable goods. Use cloth towels, napkins and nappies which can be washed, instead of disposable paper products.

41

Often, nappy services will pick up and deliver and are cheaper than using disposable nappies.

🌿 Support the recycling industry by purchasing goods that are wrapped in recycled or recyclable material. Remember, this list is only the beginning. Precycling can adapt to your life style in any way that reduces or eliminates your consumption of packaging and other resources (about 50 per cent by volume of landfill waste). The more creative you are, the better it works for you.

If you live in the UK, you may notice that some of the ideas suggested here, such as buying groceries in bulk using your own containers, are difficult to carry out in Britain. You could write to one or two supermarkets asking why they don't provide such facilities for customers.

Potential energy savings from recycling

Aluminium cans	96 per cent
Paper	70 per cent
Steel and iron	74 per cent

ACTIVITIES

Waste surveys

One way to find out how you can save waste is to make a note of everything you throw away in a week. Once you have done this, divide the items into recyclables, reusables and items that you cannot avoid throwing away. For each item ask yourself if it was really necessary to use it in the first place. You may be surprised at what you discover: I found that I could reduce my waste by around a half.

This grid will give you some idea of how to set about conducting this exercise. Some of the alternatives you think of might be a little amusing, but there is no harm in that. And you will probably find out that reducing waste and cost cutting are two sides of the same coin, so you'll save money.

Item	Reusable	Recyclable	Not needed	Alternative	Unavoidable waste
Newspaper	Maybe	Yes			
Apple core		Yes			
Paper tissues			Maybe	Cotton handker-chief?	Yes

42

Packaging survey

You could also conduct a survey among local businesses to find out their policy on packaging. You may be surprised to find out that many businesses are very positive about the idea of reducing waste. From their point of view, cutting waste can mean cutting costs and improving efficiency: an inefficient and wasteful business does not only have a greater impact on the environment, but is also less profitable. You could point out that by making attempts to improve their environmental impact they will be ahead of their competitors, and in an advantageous position once new environmental legislation comes into effect.

The important thing with local initiatives is to forge new partnerships to benefit the environment. A lot more can be achieved by cooperation than by confrontation. Even though people may not think the same way as you at the start, given time many will come to see your point of view. Sometimes, though, confrontation is the only way forward. If a company is blatantly ignoring environmental legislation or polluting the local environment with little regard to the effect of their activity, confronting them is sometimes the only way to make them see sense. I certainly favour reporting polluters to the authorities—with some people a sharp fine can be extremely beneficial to the thought processes. If you feel very strongly about an individual issue and local progress is slow, why not get involved in a national campaign? The more people show an interest, the more impetus the campaign will gather.

Contact a selected group of local businesses to represent different retail sectors. You may choose for example:

- grocery store/supermarket
- stationers
- fast food
- cosmetics store/chemist

In your survey you could ask:

What are the main types of waste/packaging in your business?
- card
- plastic
- foam
- glass
- other

What measures if any do you take to try to prevent items sold in your business from being dropped as litter?

43

❧ litter bins
❧ markings on cans, trays, etc.

Do you think that reducing packaging would affect your business? If so for what reasons?
❧ add to damage in transit
❧ make goods less appealing to consumers
❧ make handling more difficult
❧ other

Do you recycle card packaging?
What measures do you think could be taken to further reduce packaging or litter produced as a result of your business activity?

Shoppers' survey

Conduct a survey among a selected number of shoppers to complement the research among local businesses.

You might ask some of the following questions:

Which of the following methods would you favour to reduce waste/litter:
❧ additional litter-bins and recycling facilities
❧ increased use of returnable bottles
❧ increased use of recyclable materials
❧ less packaging on retail goods?

For which of the following items do you think packaging is important:
❧ vegetables
❧ electronic goods
❧ sweets
❧ fast foods
❧ cosmetics
❧ groceries (e.g. washing powder, etc)?

Do you recycle/reuse packaging?
What do you think are the main causes of litter in this area:
❧ carelessness
❧ too few litter bins
❧ lack of interest in/care for local environment
❧ other (please specify)?

Having gathered your evidence, prioritise measures which might be used to reduce the overall amount of waste/litter. You could take this further and start your own mini-campaign.

Survey work such as this is useful if you are thinking of starting your own anti-waste campaign, because it allows you to arm yourself with the statistics necessary to make your case.

Making paper

Making your own recycled paper is not a new idea, but it can be fun and you can use an interesting number of fibres, such as nettles, straw and nearly any fibrous plant. You might not end up with something you can write on, but you will find out a lot about plant fibres and their properties.

The first thing you need is a paper frame, which you can buy or make. This is simply a frame made from offcut timber and a piece of gauze. The frame consists of two halves. The bottom half is lined with gauze and the top half is open. The timber does not need to be particularly strong—anything thicker than about 1cm (½ in) should be sufficient. The gauze should have a fine mesh: you could use old, fine-net curtains. Whatever material you decide to use should be able to be fastened firmly and tightly to the frame, so cut the cloth or gauze large enough so that you can staple it in to the side (see diagram on next page) of the wood. You can also nail four thin pieces of wood on the outside of the frame to trap the gauze, which will give you a nice strong frame.

Once you have your frame, this is how to make your paper:

1 Shred your waste paper into small pieces and soak it in a bucket for a couple of hours or overnight.
2 Remove a handful of the resulting mulch from the bucket and squeeze it into a ball, removing the surplus water. Place the ball into a liquidiser with some fresh water and blend it until you have a fine purée.
3 Pour the pulp into a large plastic bowl and dilute it with warm water at a ratio of one part of pulp to one-and-a-half parts of warm water.
4 Hold the frame at the sides, with the gauze facing down, and lower it gently into the pulp. Lift it out slowly, taking care to keep it level. Allow the water to drain off, then remove the top part of the frame.
5 Spread a damp cloth on a work surface or a piece of board and turn the frame over onto the cloth. Press the gauze gently so that the pulp comes off and then cover the pulp with another drying cloth. Repeat steps 4 and 5 until you have as many pieces of paper as you require.
6 Place a board over the paper and squeeze down gently but hard. Standing on the upper board normally does the trick. This bit can be very messy, so have some absorbent material handy to catch the dripping water.

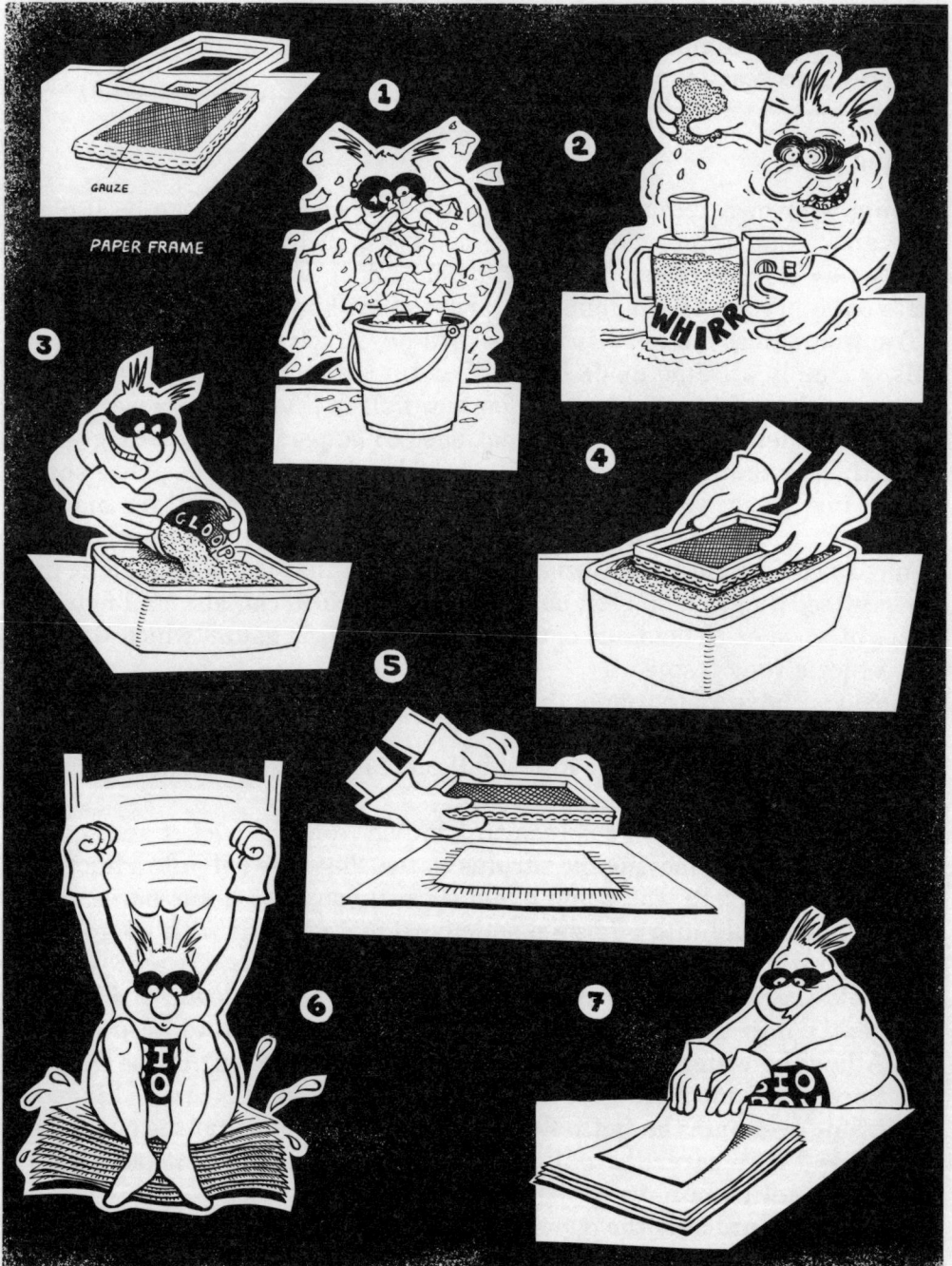

GAUZE

PAPER FRAME

7 Peel off each sheet of paper together with the drying cloth beneath it. Lay your sheets on a piece of newspaper to dry.

Experiment by mixing other types of plant fibre in with your pulp to see what difference this makes to the resulting paper. You can also try using some natural colours to dye your paper, or adding flower petals to make it decorative. Perfume can be mixed with the pulp if you want scented paper.

Note what a large quantity of water is necessary to make paper. The reason that making recycled paper uses less energy than making paper from virgin pulp is that used paper is a lot easier to make into a pulp than timber—just imagine trying to liquidise a few solid branches.

3   Habitats

The natural world is an unending source of adventure and investigation. It is startling in its beauty and sometimes its brutality. Yet the natural world is self-regulating and allows the development of a remarkably stable relationship between species. Its complexities are never-ending and never fail to fascinate. Few areas of study could provide a better backdrop for our investigation into the world about us.

Helping to preserve rare species is one of the most exciting and rewarding areas of conservation work. Many superb schemes have helped to hold back some of the ravages of the twentieth century, but there is still an enormous amount to do if our rich natural heritage is to survive far into the next. It is easy to become depressed by statistics which show rainforest disappearing at a rate equivalent to a football pitch per second and deserts spreading faster than ever before, but getting depressed will not solve the enormous problems facing our natural world. What can help are practical conservation measures, and getting involved in helping the wildlife in your area. You may also support some of the excellent environmental groups around the world, such as the World Wide Fund for Nature or Greenpeace, who are in the business of getting things going politically.

BIODIVERSITY

Building habitats that are likely to benefit a wide range of natural species is often referred to as encouraging biodiversity. Understanding which plants are likely to encourage wildlife is often central to this process.

48

Why human beings are important

Wildlife has often been viewed in relation to the place of species within natural systems. Traditional textbooks have examined ecosystems in terms of species interdependence, concentrating on how species relate to one another in natural environments. The relationship between human beings and animals has traditionally been studied under the heading of human influences or impacts on ecosystems. In my view this emphasis is misleading: human beings have been around for some four million years, and in that time they have played a role in the development of nearly all natural systems. The world's rainforests, for example, are often regarded as one of the few remaining truly natural habitats. They are home, however, to millions of people. Many rainforest peoples have lived in harmony with the natural system around them for time out of mind. Some animals and plants have become dependent on habitats created and shaped by human beings. In some cases the removal of human influences would be disastrous for wildlife, as for instance where wildlife communities have developed around coppiced woods or hedges in Europe.

A better way of looking at habitats and the way they are influenced by our activities is by examining them in terms of change. As a general rule of thumb, sudden change is not favourable for wildlife, and it takes a while for new species to appear when conditions have become unfavourable for others. While it is pretty obvious that replacing a jungle with a road will be disastrous in wildlife terms, more subtle changes to habitats can also affect wildlife almost as drastically. It is often the case that the decline of one species or other is due to a range of different factors, such as competition from other species coupled with pollution, habitat loss and so on. In almost every case, human beings are an important part of the picture. Conservation schemes need to take the human factor into account in order to have a chance of long-term success. Keeping human beings as a part of the picture can help preserve wildlife habitats. It is neither possible nor desirable to fence areas of the world off from people in order to preserve wildlife, but it is possible to involve local communities in a way which both benefits them and protects the environment.

Wildlife tourism

For developing countries, attracting tourists to see local wildlife is an expanding area. In 1994, the new multiracial government in South Africa announced that it was to expand its tourist programme. Wildlife tourism was seen as an important area for development. Because South Africa is a beautiful country with many unique wildlife habitats, the idea has massive potential. Almost as soon as the announcement was made, however, speculation began as to whether developing this type of tourism might endanger the very wildlife it set out to promote.

The problem with wildlife tourism is that it is often followed by rapid commercial development in areas surrounding and within natural sanctuaries. This can be damaging, but that need not be the case. With planning, tourism can be managed so that it does not harm wildlife; indeed, it can actually help to encourage governments to protect valuable conservation areas.

Some of the best examples of sensitive wildlife tourism are to be found in Kenya, where tourism has become an important source of income. Around 10 per cent of the country is now used as wildlife parks and reserves. Tourism is the largest source of foreign income, bringing in an estimated £180 million ($270 million) per year.

In Tsavo national park, planning helped to ensure that hotels were built outside sensitive areas. Regular meetings between park staff and government officials meant that essential information was incorporated in the decision-making process. Such careful planning has helped to make Tsavo a success in both tourism and wildlife terms. Like Tsavo, many of Kenya's wildlife parks have buffer zones to keep tourist development away from sensitive conservation zones.

The table below outlines some of the differences between good and bad tourism.

Good tourism	Bad tourism
Meetings between park managers and government	Government fails to listen to park managers
Hotels built outside area of national park	Hotels built within national park
Buffer zones set up around national park	Too many tourists visiting sensitive areas

The Periyar wildlife sanctuary in India

The Periyar wildlife sanctuary in southern India is home to around 40 tigers, more than 800 elephants and a huge variety of other animals and plants. Periyar is interesting because it shows how an area can recover from being developed and once again become home to wild animals and plants.

In 1895 a huge dam was built in Periyar, and about 55 square kilometres of some of the best wildlife habitat in India were destroyed. Today, however, a sanctuary of 780 square kilometres has been declared, as one of 16 Project Tiger reserves in India run with help from the World Wide Fund for Nature. In 1900 there were more than 40,000 tigers in India but by 1962 less than 200 animals survived, thanks mostly to hunting for sport and furs. Today the tiger is protected in places such as Periyar, and India now has around 4,000 of them.

At Periyar, the reservoir now provides a source of fresh water for the animals, and its presence has helped keep the human population of this area far lower than in most areas of southern India, which is one of the most densely populated parts of the subcontinent. The park attracts more than 150,000 tourists every year, so it is an important place for the local economy.

It is not always an easy job protecting this magnificent wildlife sanctuary from poaching and overgrazing by cattle. Conservationists try to avoid overgrazing by talking to local farmers and making certain that too many cattle aren't put on a single area. Cattle can also introduce disease into wildlife areas: in Periyar in 1974–5 more than 1,000 herbivores died from rinderpest, a sickness spread by cattle. Now cows in the surrounding area are vaccinated against this disease.

Sanctuaries or partnerships?

Designating areas as wildlife sanctuaries is useful for protecting threatened species such as the tiger which has a range of up to 10,360 hectares (40 square miles) for a breeding pair, so need plenty of space. But all land has conservation value, so ideally conservation should feature in all planning and countryside management. Sensitive land management programmes should take into account the requirements of local wildlife, as well as the needs of local farmers and developers. That is why what you do in your own back yard is just as important as helping to protect species in the far-off reaches of the world. Ideally we should see our relationship with the natural world as a partnership; if this were the case there would be less need to hive off areas for special protection. Conservation measures should be considered before an animal becomes endangered—not afterwards, when it is probably already too late.

In eastern Australia a new project to protect the country's most famous marsupial—the koala—aims to do just that. In New South Wales koalas are on the list of threatened species for the first time, and their nationwide numbers have declined from around 400,000 in 1986 to less than 100,000 today. The main reason for this decline is habitat loss due to factors such as farming and housing development, and, more surprisingly, through attacks by domestic dogs. In addition, a bacterium called *chlamydia psittaci*, which causes diseases such as conjunctivitis, is also a threat. By encouraging councils to leave pockets of trees and conserve areas where the koala lives, it is hoped that the decline in koalas can be checked.

Take action

Find out more about wildlife in your own area, and what can be done to protect it. You can do this by contacting a local conservation organisation or one of those listed at the end of this book. Or you might want to start your own conservation area (see end of chapter).

The spread of the deserts

One-third of the earth's land surface is arid or semi-arid, yet is home to more than 600 million people. More than one-sixth of the earth's land surface is under threat from desertification. The causes of spreading deserts include overgrazing, growing too many crops, removal of trees for firewood and climate change. Desertification is one of the world's most serious environmental problems: millions of people and animals are put at risk of starvation as fragile lands lose their fertility. Sub-Saharan Africa is one of the most threatened regions—here overgrazing has often combined with drought, with devastating results for people and environment alike.

Can desertification be stopped?

The spread of deserts can be checked by using different methods which mainly aim to stop sands shifting. Common methods include building terraces, laying lines of brushwood and planting trees. Planting specially improved crops can also help. Good crop management is very important in areas such as northern Nigeria, on the edge of the Sahel, where soils are particularly liable to erosion. One of the biggest problems is that many arid areas are very remote, and helping people to learn how to control the desert is not easy. However, many aid agencies are helping with local programmes to stop desertification. If you are interested in finding out more, contact one of the agencies working in this area such as Oxfam (for addresses, see the back of the book).

Forestry

The world's forests are one of our most precious wildlife sanctuaries. Many of our wild animals and plants live on, or at, the fringes of forests. Forests cover around a third of the earth's land area, they are a valuable resource influencing global climate, environment, wildlife habitat and biodiversity. They are important sources of timber and firewood. They are renewable resources: if timber extraction is balanced with planting and management programmes, the same area of land can be used almost indefinitely for growing trees. Yet on a global scale, the area of land under forest cover has been in continuous decline for hundreds of years. This deforestation can cause severe problems such as flooding, soil erosion, the spread of deserts, the decline in soil productivity and famine. Much of it can be traced to the development of human settlement and the spread of agriculture, with some impact from other factors such as climatic change. By and large, as societies have developed, deforestation has tended to accelerate.

Rates of forest loss are startling. Each year 12 million hectares (30 million acres) are cleared for agriculture and fuel, and a further 4.5 million hectares (11 million acres) are cut in commercial logging. Even though some forests are being planted, there continues to be a net loss overall.

Many factors, including social, economic and demographic considerations, affect the rate of forest loss. For example, although the world's tropical forests are under enormous pressure, the area of coniferous forest in the northern hemisphere has increased through new planting and regeneration. In the United Kingdom, the area of forest doubled between 1919 and 1994, from 5 per cent to 10 per cent of the country's land area, but this is still far lower than the figure for mainland Europe of 25 per cent.

Commercial forestry

One of the problems of commercial forestry is that it often tends to concentrate on the production of one or two fast-growing species, which are often not native to the areas where they are planted. In some cases, rare wildlife habitats have been removed in order to make way for commercial timber plantations in a kind of eco-vandalism, similar to that of ripping up existing native woodlands.

In developing countries particularly, planting programmes have often gone ahead with little notice being taken of the needs of local peoples (see Chapter 1). While it is difficult to see how the world's demand for timber can be met without some kind of commercial plantations, the introduction of diverse native species into an area is likely to provide the best option for wildlife. Corridors of native species running through forests increase the forest's conservation value. In the UK the multipurpose management of forests now includes the planting of native species, often along roads and streams, as well as the development of recreational facilities.

Forests and the greenhouse effect

The destruction of forests does not only have consequences for wildlife, but for the environment as a whole. Trees store carbon dioxide from photosynthesis, and this represents a significant pool on a global basis. When forests are removed, this carbon dioxide is eventually released into the atmosphere, adding to global climate change. Conversely, planting trees can have a beneficial effect by removing carbon dioxide, the main greenhouse gas, from the atmosphere (see Chapter 7). Thus, by planting trees it is possible to compensate for the global production of CO_2. Unfortunately, this is not an answer to the problem of global warming because it would not be practical to plant the vast number of trees necessary even to begin to offset CO_2 emissions. In the UK it has been estimated that one million hectares (2.5 million acres) of new forest would remove less than 3 per cent of the country's carbon dioxide production, and an interesting study in the USA by Applied Energy Services, an independent power company, has estimated that planting 52 million trees in Guatemala over a period of ten years would be sufficient to absorb the CO_2 emissions for 40 years of one 80-megawatt, coal-fired power station that it is building in Connecticut. However, planting trees still has a role in an overall package aimed at tackling global warming.

TROPICAL RAINFORESTS

'Its lands are high; there are in it very many sierras and very lofty mountains. . . . All are most beautiful, of a thousand shapes; all are accessible and filled with trees of a thousand kinds and tall, so that they seem to touch the sky. I am told that they never lose their foliage, and this I can believe, for I saw them as green and lovely as they are in Spain in May, and some of them were flowering, some bearing fruit and some at another stage, according to their nature.'

So wrote Christopher Columbus in 1492 on first landing on the island of

Hispaniola, now Haiti and the Dominican Republic. Columbus' wonder at the beauty of the forests of the West Indies is not surprising. Few places on earth are as special as tropical rainforests, because of their spectacular diversity and the unique nature of many of the plants and animals living in them. Rainforests are among the oldest habitats on earth—some may be up to 100 million years old. In other words, rainforests have existed since dinosaurs roamed the earth. The threat facing these magnificent places has received much publicity in the last few years, yet despite this high profile, rainforests and the problems that surround them are still widely misunderstood. So where are the rainforests and why is it important to preserve them?

Rainforests are found in three main areas of the world: South and Central America; western and Central Africa and Madagascar; Southeast Asia, the Pacific Islands and northern Australia. Many are located in developing nations, where they sometimes represent one of the main natural resources available for exploitation. Rainforest soils are poor and not much good for agriculture, but in some areas they contain rich deposits of tin and aluminium ore, called borax. It is sometimes pointed out that the developed nations—many of whom cut down their forests hundreds of years ago— have little right to tell developing nations what to do with theirs, so it is important to look at our attitude to natural resources when dealing with issues like rainforests. Promoting sustainable development involves the developed nations just as much as it does the developing ones, we need to critically evaluate the way we deal with our own natural resources as a first step.

Rainforests are a very particular type of forest. Technically the term only applies to those habitats that receive four metres of rain a year or more; but many areas on the fringes of rainforests which receive less rain, two to four metres (72 to 144 inches) a year are often categorised as tropical rainforests. Strictly speaking, they are tropical moist forests.

The value of rainforests

Tropical rainforests are not only a resource for wildlife, but are a resource for the entire human race. These habitats are priceless natural sanctuaries and are invaluable gene pools, containing many rare species which could be used to develop future sources of food and medicine. It has been estimated that rainforests contain up to half of the world's plants and animals, even though they only cover around 7 per cent of the earth's land area.

A typical four-mile stretch of Amazonian rainforest contains up to 1,500 species of plant, including 750 species of trees, 400 species of birds, and

Rainforests have three distinct habitat layers: 1) The high treetops, 2) the main forest canopy, 3) ground level. Each supports a huge range of animal and plant life.

250 species of mammals. Rainforests contain so many different insects that biologists have a long way to go to identify them all. Discoveries of new species are made almost every year—recently a new species of oryx, a type of antelope, was found in Vietnam, despite the dreadful defoliation that country has suffered. The tragedy of rainforests is that many of their species may never be discovered.

The plants and animals of the rainforests include some of the world's rarest and most unusual species. Exotic orchids, climbers and epiphytes—plants growing in trees—dwell in the forests, together with many large and colourful butterflies and birds. Species in danger of extinction include the jaguar, the woolly spider monkey and the scarlet macaw. The golden lion tamarin of South America is one of the rarest animals on earth. Species such as the giant atlas moth in Southeast Asia and the world's largest and most smelly flower, *Rafflesia arnoldii*, in Sumatra are also rapidly disappearing. In Southeast Asia, the once common tiger is now also an endangered species. Unfortunately many species have already become extinct.

Tribal peoples

As well as this remarkable range of plants and animals, millions of people depend on the world's rainforests. Like the habitat itself, the tribal peoples of the world are also fighting a battle for survival. Between 1900 and 1989, Brazil lost 89 tribes, an average of one a year. Many peoples have been deliberately killed and their lands taken; others have been resettled in unfamiliar areas, or ended up landless and destitute.

Yet tribal peoples have a greater claim to rainforest lands than anyone. They lived in the forests long before Europeans ever set foot in them, and their rich and varied cultures have survived unchanged for thousands of years. All aspects of the native people's lives, including their religions, are based on the forest. They know more about the ways of the rainforest than any other people on earth.

Tribal peoples practise a sustainable type of agriculture, clearing small patches of forest for food crops such as rice, sago and cassava, or tapioca. Because these 'farm plots' are small and are left for long periods before being used again, the forest is able to recover. These plots often support a startling variety of plants: in the Philippines, the Hanunco people are familiar with 420 crops, growing as many as 40 together in two-acre areas.

The Lacondon Indians

The Lacondon Indians of Mexico grow up to 80 crops on a single plot, using their knowledge of the rainforest to maximise yields and prevent erosion. The Lacondon choose a plot according to the type of soil, using only three of the seven types of soil they distinguish. At the beginning of the year they clear one or two hectares of rainforest, leaving the trees and vegetation to dry for burning in April. In tropical rainforests most of the nutrients are stored in the plants, so burning the forest creates a rich ash to fertilise the Lacondon crops. Fast-growing trees such as papaya and banana are planted to prevent erosion and to provide shade. Then the Lacondon plant a range of root crops, followed by their staple cereal, maize, and around 60 to 80 other crops. Every two or three years, they move to new areas, allowing the rainforest to recover.

It is well worth finding out more about the plight of the world's tribal peoples. You can do so by contacting or joining one of the organisations fighting for their survival, such as Survival International. Several excellent books also cover the subject, including *In the Rainforest* by Catherine Caufield.

Food and medicines

Many of the world's food plants—including coffee, tea, tomatoes, bananas, pineapple, avocados, maize, cocoa, rice and Brazil nuts—originate from tropical forests. Though most of these crops are now grown in plantations, plants from the wild are important for breeding as many have qualities which become lost in cultivated varieties, such as resistance to disease. Because rainforest habitats are so rich, they produce a far higher total yield from native species than the same land does if used for ranching, agriculture or commercial plantations. Traditional rainforest occupations include collecting Brazil nuts and rubber tapping. By collecting the natural fruits in this way, the rainforest can be used as a sustainable resource.

Drugs extracted from topical forest plants have been used in almost every branch of Western medicine. Atropine, which is obtained from the Jimson weed, is used to treat eye infections; the same plant yields hyocine, used as a sedative and to treat travel sickness. Benzoin, from a South American tree, is used to treat bronchitis and laryngitis. And only a tiny proportion of tropical forest plants have ever been tested for their medical properties, so many more medicines may lie undiscovered in rainforests.

Life cycle of the forest

Although rainforests are rich in species, their soils are mostly infertile. Dead plant material rots down five times faster in the humid environment than in cooler climates. Rainforest plants have shallow roots, and the nutrients released from rotting materials are quickly absorbed again by the plants, rather than building up in the soil.

The effects of deforestation

Rainforests grow in hot and wet parts of the world, which are subject to periods of heavy rain and intense heat, conditions in which the forests stabilise the climate and provide an ideal environment for plants and animals. Deforestation causes problems with the local climate—the area becomes hotter and dryer.

Soil erosion

When forests are removed the thin topsoil is quickly washed away and soil nutrients rapidly depleted. In these conditions, land soon becomes unproductive. In rainforests only a small amount of soil need be eroded to have a

58

severe effect on soil fertility, and in countries such as Madagascar and Brazil, erosion of rainforest soils is widespread.

Sometimes deforested soils form a crust during periods of heavy rain, which then can become so hard that water cannot penetrate it. The result is that plants can fail through drought even though tropical rainforests are among the wettest areas on earth. At the same time, flash floods occur because the water can no longer be absorbed into the soil but runs off straight into the rivers.

MYTH-BUSTERS

Rainforests are the lungs of the earth

A rainforest is a balanced system, absorbing about the same amount of carbon dioxide as it produces. However, rainforests represent an important carbon sink. When burned, they give off the CO_2 stored in the trees, adding to global warming. Rainforests also have an important role in maintaining stability in the local climate, and in the local water cycle. A better slogan than 'the lungs of the world' would be 'the life-blood of the tropics'—without the forests many tropical areas end up becoming little better than deserts.

Settlement

Every year large numbers of landless settlers move into areas such as the Amazon and clear rainforest. These are mainly poor people whose aim is simply to make a living. Since most rainforest soils are not suited to growing agricultural crops for long periods of time, the land becomes infertile after a few years and the settlers move on further and further into the forest. From space, vast plumes of smoke can be seen rising from many of the world's rainforests, marking all the fires lit by settlers to clear new patches of land.

Logging

Every year around 5.6 million hectares (12.5 million acres) of rainforest are destroyed or damaged by logging. In countries such as Malaysia nearly all destruction is caused that way. Sometimes only the valuable trees such as mahogany are removed, but at others all the trees are cut down. Even when some trees are left behind, enormous damage is done to the forest. Huge tracks have to be cut to allow the trees to be removed, and heavy machinery has to be used to transport the fallen trees. Forests can take hundreds of years to recover from this type of damage.

Roads and development

Modern technology has greatly accelerated the rate of rainforest destruction. By 1989 an estimated 50 per cent of the world's tropical forests had been lost, 10 per cent of it in the ten years between 1979 and 1989. New roads such as the Trans-Amazonian highway have been built, which allow armies of landless settlers to move easily into once-remote areas to clear the forests. In the Amazon, much of the land has subsequently been used for cattle ranching or land speculation.

Debt

One reason why it is difficult for countries with tropical rainforests to stop the destruction is debt. Many countries simply cannot afford programmes to protect the forest; others need the money they obtain from selling timber. For example, the current Brazilian debt is approximately $110 billion, most of which is owed to the rich Western nations. Promoting a more equitable trading environment would certainly benefit developing nations.

Can the rainforests recover?

Areas of land affected by deforestation can recover if given a chance. Secondary forest growth—the first stages of recovery—occurs quickly in some parts of the world. In other areas, planting programmes can allow existing areas of forest to be reconnected, providing corridors for wildlife to move around. In the Atlantic rainforest in Brazil, for example, the extent of deforestation means that this may be the only way of saving some species.

The Atlantic rainforest is among the most endangered ecosystem in South America, and certainly the most threatened natural resource in Brazil. The forest stretches across almost the entire Atlantic coast of Brazil, extending into Argentina and Paraguay. In the south of the region is an area of Araucaria forest (a family of trees which includes the monkey puzzle). This, like so much in the Atlantic rainforest, is unique. The area also contains a variety of coastal and seasonal forests. One of the problems for conservation is that this once vast ecosystem, which used to occupy around 12 per cent of the land area of Brazil, has become fragmented. Many of the species living there are now isolated in small pockets. This has the effect of making them doubly endangered, partly because they exist in very small numbers and

60

also because they have no means of migrating to adjacent areas in the event of disasters such as floods or climate change. Predators such as large cats (of which there are many different species in the region) are particularly at risk.

Conservation in the Atlantic rainforest has concentrated on co-ordinating community efforts in the three countries in the region. Two measures that are very promising are the planting of corridors joining smaller areas of forest, and conserving the top carnivores (which has the effect of also protecting many of the smaller species which, as I have explained earlier, generally require much smaller areas in which to live). Public campaigns combined with environmental education have helped make the people in the area far more aware of the issues. Atlantic rainforest conservation efforts include many community schemes, and over the years these have proved their worth in bringing about successful conservation. Although the Atlantic rainforest is still endangered, the success to date of the many schemes should not be underestimated. The challenge now is to initiate more community schemes throughout the world, concentrating on rare habitats, while supporting the efforts in areas such as the Brazilian Atlantic forest.

Reforestation programmes often require between 20 and 40 years to make a real mark, but given time and space many species of plant and animal can make a comeback. All the same, it could take centuries to repair some of the damage caused by deforestation—and reforestation is no good to those species that have already been made extinct.

Preserving rainforests

Many good schemes now exist to protect rainforests, but much more still needs to be done. Some countries have declared areas of rainforest as national parks, but most rainforests are still unprotected. Controlling the export of timber from tropical areas could help to save some forests. Much could be done to give tropical countries a better deal and help save rainforests by writing off international debts or investing in schemes designed to protect the forest.

Take action

- ❧ Ask your local timber merchant to stock only hardwoods from substainably managed forests.
- ❧ Avoid purchasing products made from tropical timber where at all possible. Consider alternatives such as products made from ash, beech and oak.

61

🌿 Reuse or recycle discarded timber or furniture.

🌿 Support organisations fighting to save tropical forests and their peoples.

AGRICULTURE

Modern agricultural methods have led to a massive increase in the world's food-producing capacity. But this progress, unfortunately, has often been paid for by environmental degradation. Thus short-term gain has led to a longer-term threat to the world's food supply. The challenge facing the world's farmers is to retain food-producing capacity while attempting to protect the environment. This could be achieved in a number of different ways. For example, farmers could produce less in total, but these food resources could be used more efficiently so that a higher proportion of the food produced enters the human food chain.

The problems that farmers face are, to say the least, complex. In developing countries the pressure placed on poor, marginal land can be enormous. In some developed parts of the world intensification has equally led to the degradation of land.

In either case the environment, and the people that rely on it, lose out. In some countries, rich and productive habitats have been removed to make way for farms which produce a fraction of the capacity of the natural habitat they replace. In such situations progress is often best made through working with individual farmers to develop methods that fit in with the ecological, structural and physical constraints of the area concerned.

Modern farming methods

Covering huge areas with just one or two crops can lead to the creation of wildlife deserts. By rotating crops and leaving suitable niches for wildlife, chemical inputs can be reduced and wild species encouraged. From an environmental point of view, mixed farming is usually better than intensive systems which concentrate on the growth of one or two crops or the keeping of a particular kind of livestock. Many arable fields receive little or no organic manure, while livestock farmers have a considerable problem disposing of animal wastes without causing pollution. In Belgium, the government has set targets for the reduction of the country's manure mountain. You might laugh at the idea, but the problem is a serious one.

Take action

Write to one or two agrochemical companies and ask them what they do to ensure that their products do not cause pollution or harm wildlife. You might point to a single issue, such as asking what they are doing about the pollution of ground water by nitrates (see Chapter 6). It is also worth asking what the company's policy is on marketing products to developing countries. Ask if they will send you a list of products they market overseas.

Many companies produce glossy brochures to sell their point of view, so it is worth writing to an organic growers' association, the Soil Association or organisations such as Friends of the Earth that work on this issue and comparing notes. Try to find out the ecological effects of a range of compounds marketed by the company. Consider whether the claimed benefits are worth the environmental costs. If you disagree with what any companies say about their products, write and let them know. If you can visit some farms, it is well worth doing so, especially if you can compare, for example, an organic farm with a mixed and an intensive arable farm. Consider the economic and other pressures that different types of farms are under, and try and work out the underlying reasons for them. Once you have all the

63

information, make up your own mind on the issues concerned and write up your project, including any conclusions.

You can encourage organic methods of growing by purchasing organic foodstuffs. If you know a good farm, it is worth buying their products at the farm shop.

THE WILDLIFE COLLECTORS

Botanic collections—Kew Gardens

Botanical research might not to seem to be at the cutting edge of saving the environment. However, botanical collections such as Kew Gardens in London allow valuable research into plants, which is vital for conservation work. The collection at Kew began over 200 years ago, long before environmental issues became fashionable. Today, as well as holding samples of some of the world's rarest plants, it holds one of the most important collections of seeds on earth, which are not only valuable from a scientific point of view but can also be used in reintroduction programmes.

Although collections such as those at Kew are extremely important, many conservationists believe that our greatest efforts should go into protecting species in the wild. If you are interested in plants, you should certainly never remove rare plants from their native site. A collection of photographs is a far better record of your discoveries than a series of damaged habitats.

Zoos

Zoos are a legacy of the last century, when collecting wild animals was fashionable and attitudes to nature were different (see Chapter 1). Today, there are two prevailing attitudes towards them. Some people see zoos as important conservation sites offering a refuge for endangered species. Others see them as detracting from the real business of protecting wildlife habitats, and as leading to the exploitation of creatures in the wild by encouraging the trade in animals. Both views have some basis in truth. Some zoos are indeed engaged in valuable conservation work, while others keep animals in the most appalling conditions and are little more than examples of human exploitation and cruelty to wild species. The trade in wild animals has led to untold suffering, particularly among primate species and exotic birds. International efforts to ban some of the worst practices have helped, but illegal wildlife trading still poses a threat to endangered species in many parts of the world. Even previously unidentified species have been captured by wildlife poachers. Recently in Indonesia, for example,

64

two new species of finch were found in tiny cages—but both birds were dead.

It is unfortunate, but as matters stand, zoos probably offer the best chance for many endangered species. From a conservation point of view, however, it remains far better to protect animals in the wild than to place them in cages as exhibits. If you are interested in promoting the conservation work of zoos and helping to stop the trade in wild animals, I would recommend that you get in touch with one of the agencies working in this area, such as Zoo Check.

ACTIVITIES

Tropical forest survey

Have a look around your own home to discover how many objects are made from items originating either directly or indirectly from rainforests. Some of the wooden items might be quite difficult to identify, because manufacturers do not advertise the fact that their products are made from timber extracted from rainforest. You can assume that most exotic hardwood products use rainforest timber, unless the manufacturer advertises otherwise.

Here's a list to get you going. It might contain a few surprises: aluminium items (many rainforest areas have rich borax deposits); rubber items; bananas; maize (cornflakes, for example); tomatoes; a wide variety of hardwood-timber items including mahogany; palm oil; chewing gum; balsam; Brazil nuts; sugar; rice; many houseplants, including Swiss Cheese plants (*Monstera deliciosa*) and other philodendrons, begonias, rubber plants (*Ficus elastica*), peperomia and many, many others; parrots and many other cage-birds; a huge variety of drugs.

If you want to convince anyone that rainforests are valuable resources for human beings as well as wildlife, get them to try this activity too. Make a note of the number of food products you eat in one day that use rainforest products: look out for many breakfast cereals, biscuits, margarines—which include palm oil or annatto—and many desserts.

There is a number of experiments you can try to find out the effect of a rainforest on the local climate. Here's one idea that is quite enjoyable.

1. Take two seed trays. Fill both with a sandy seed compost, or mix your own using two parts horticultural-grade sand to one part seed compost (many rainforest soils are light and sandy).
2. Evenly sow about 24 tomato seeds in one of the trays and cover with a thin layer of compost. Leave the other tray unsown.
3. Keep both trays moist until the seedlings grow.

4. When the seedlings are about 7 cm high, try watering both trays with a large amount of water, to simulate torrential rain.
5. Note what happens to the surface soil in each case. You should be able to deduce what happens to rainforest soils if the trees are removed.

Once the soil has had a chance to dry out, try placing both trays in a sunny position and measure the temperature on the surface in the middle of each tray. You should record a lower temperature on the tray with the seedlings, because the seedlings lose water through their leaves through a process called evapotranspiration, and this cools the surrounding area a little. On a larger scale, the shading effect of plants is also a factor in sunny weather. Deforested areas tend to be hotter and dryer than areas covered by rainforests.

Making a worm bin

A good way to compost your kitchen waste is by using a worm bin. Various worms are suitable for compost-making, including brandling worms (*Eisenia foetida*), which are little trouble to keep and can be left unfed for several weeks. The worm bin should be placed in a warm, sheltered spot, out of full sunshine. A worm bin is not smelly, so you can even keep it inside during winter.

You can make your own worm bin easily with a few household items:

❀ Plastic dustbin or compost bin
❀ Sand or gravel

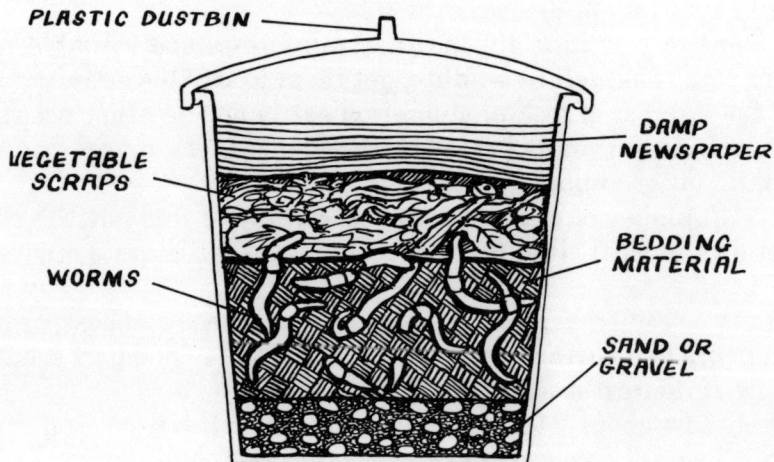

66

- Bedding material such as shredded newspaper mixed with leafmould— it should be damp
- Suitable worms (around half a yoghurt pot full)
- vegetable scraps
- damp newspaper

Place a 15-cm (six-inch) layer of sand or gravel at the base of the bin to provide drainage. Place the bedding material on top, and introduce the worms. Place around 1 litre of kitchen scraps in one corner of the bin and wait until this is well colonised before adding more in another part of the bin. This may take a few weeks when the bin is new, but will speed up as the worms breed. If too much food is added at first it will putrefy before the worms have a chance to eat it. Cover the compost with a layer of damp newspaper—because worms breathe through their skins, they do not like dry conditions. Once you get your worm bin going properly, you can regularly throw your kitchen vegetable scraps into the bin to provide food. The worms will gradually process this waste into a very useful soil conditioner. If you do not have a garden, you can use the resulting compost for growing houseplants or give it to your friends.

4 The Home and Garden— an Invisible World

It is easy to forget in the comfort of your own home that you are surrounded by millions of other forms of life. Insects, fungi and bacteria tend to be seen as a nuisance to be avoided or destroyed. However, our own bodies contain hundreds of different varieties of perfectly harmless, and in many cases useful, bacteria. Much of the food we eat contains bacteria or fungi of different types, many of which are added deliberately during processing. Cheese, yoghurt and alcoholic drinks are the obvious examples that fall into this category, but there are many others such as yeast extract.

Wherever we live it is unavoidable that we share our habitat with a range of other species, many of which we are not even aware of. Most other forms of life, even the vast majority of bacteria or fungi, do not pose a threat to human beings. In fact, a great deal of pleasure can be gained from watching the area around your home once you realise that very little of what you see is likely to be harmful. Even if you don't have a garden of your own, you can encourage insect species such as bees.

It is sometimes surprising how many habitats exist in urban environments, perhaps because we tend to associate city areas only with people. Even some quite rare species, including predatory birds, have found niches in towns. Although factors such as air pollution and water pollution limit the colonisation of many areas, it remains true that many animals and plants can and do live in cities. While some species scavenge for food, others have found a foothold in nature areas and parks.

It is impossible to build anything like complete ecosystems in cities, because the urban landscape is simply too domesticated, but a wide range of species can be encouraged. The average suburban garden can provide a refuge for around 30 different bird species, more than 20 insect species and up to 20 species of butterfly and moth, not to mention small mammals, snakes, lizards, frogs and slow-worms. A recent survey of Buckingham Palace Gardens in the heart of London found that the garden had 21 species of nesting birds, 343 species of butterfly and moth—about 10 per cent of all species native to the United Kingdom—57 species of spider and 90 different beetles.

Buckingham Palace Gardens are huge, but no matter how small your garden you can make an effort to encourage a broad range of species. In order to do this you need to recognise what encourages wildlife: our gardens are themselves part of the broader ecosystem, and semi-wild areas rich with native herbaceous plants, shrubs and trees will provide a far richer habitat than a conventional lawn and flowerbed. If you plan carefully, you can create a diverse habitat without the garden looking scruffy. One of the best ways of doing this is by screening off the semi-wild areas and choosing shrubs that are both attractive and encourage wildlife.

Sometimes people express concern that there may be species you do not want to encourage, such as rats or poisonous snakes—although it is worth bearing in mind that most snakes are very shy, and in Europe at least there are very few poisonous species. The best advice is that, if you know a certain species is a problem in your area, avoid creating habitats that will attract it. As a general rule, do not put meat products on compost heaps: they encourage flies and rats.

But, overall, I have never known a nature garden attract many harmful species. Indeed, a garden with a balanced habitat will often contain fewer insect pests, because it will also contain a variety of predators that keep pests down naturally. In a balanced ecosystem, so-called pests are actually important food sources for predators. Many pests are regarded as such only because they have found niches in human environments. We need to ask ourselves, 'What is a pest?' Take snakes, for example. They have a very bad image, but it is usually quite unfair. Partly because of our attitude towards them, many wild snakes are becoming endangered or even facing extinction. It is worth keeping an open mind before branding one species or another as a pest.

One of the main places that wildlife can be encouraged is on the fringes of urban areas, where woodlands can not only provide a sanctuary for wildlife but can also be used for recreation. These woodland areas can be extended into the city or to existing woods, thus providing corridors for wildlife.

CHEMICALS IN THE GARDEN

Gardeners in the last century did not have the range of chemicals available to us today, and yet they managed to grow a wide variety of ornamental plants, fruit and vegetables without trouble. How was this so? They used natural methods of pest control such as rotation, and the placing of barriers such as netting over the most vulnerable crops. Today there are more than 100 different chemicals available for gardeners in a wide range of formulations. Some of these chemicals have turned out to be highly poisonous, not only for the pest species that they are supposed to attack but also for other species, including human beings. Perhaps the best known example of a poisonous pesticide is DDT, a chemical widely used for pest control throughout the world until the 1970s, with devastating effects.

Many other chemical pesticides have since proved to be harmful to wildlife. Many agents kill off insect predators as well as pest species, making infestation even more likely. In addition, many pest species have been able to develop tolerance to new chemicals. Although DDT and a number of other persistent chemicals have been banned in developed nations, many of these substances are still used in developing countries. Some of these compounds could enter fragile ecosystems and cause a lot of damage.

The careful use of beneficial insects makes it possible to control many pests biologically without incurring the risks inherent in pesticides. Anyone who has used chemicals in gardening and then switched to organic methods can tell you the effects. For the first year or so you may see an increase in the number of pest species, but as the numbers of predators in the garden increase so the pest attack decreases. And switching to organic growing need not be painful at all, as there are many natural ways of controlling pests during that first year without resorting to chemicals. If all else fails there is a number of natural substances such as derris which can be used.

Here are a few hints to get you going with an organic garden: Avoid artificial fertilisers; instead use natural substances such as farmyard manure, home-made compost and liquid seaweed to feed plants. A wide range of organic fertilisers is available in most garden centres and horticultural stores. Natural substances have the added effect of enriching soils as well as feeding plants, so over a number of years you should see an increase in earthworms and other soil fauna. Natural manures also help increase a soil's water-holding capacity and are less easily washed out of the soils into rivers and watercourses (see Chapter 6).

Avoid using garden chemicals; where you have no choice, use natural substances. There is a variety of physical barriers you can use in order to prevent pest attack. Fine mesh netting is effective against butterflies and

70

moths, and also useful in preventing attack by birds. This technique is particularly useful for protecting members of the cabbage (or brassica) family such as cabbage, cauliflower and broccoli. A small bowl full of beer or another sweet liquid can be used to trap slugs and snails.

Encourage frogs, toads and small mammals such as hedgehogs in your garden. These species eat slugs and snails and are remarkably beneficial for the organic gardener.

If you must use pesticides, avoid what is called insurance spraying, when you spray to prevent pest attack rather than cure it. Find out about the chemicals you are using, and try to buy the less persistent ones. Avoid residual weedkillers which stay in the ground and continue to kill weeds over a period of months. A number of these can get in to water supplies, as well as damaging the soil for a considerable period. Avoid breathing in spray and wash your hands carefully after spraying. Store chemicals out of reach of young children. And spray against pest attack only as a very last resort. Once you have developed a rich fauna in your garden, pest attack becomes far less of a problem.

INVESTIGATE BENEFICIAL INSECTS

Find out more about beneficial insects in your area. The species vary from country to country, but it is worth remembering that nearly all pest species have natural enemies, and by encouraging these you can discourage pests.

Beneficial insects in commercial horticulture

Two beneficial minibeasts which have found favour in commercial horticulture are *Encarsia formosa*, a tiny species of parasitic wasp, and *Phytosiulis persemilis*, a predatory mite. These are enemies of two of the worst glasshouse pests, whitefly and red spider mite respectively. *Encarsia formosa* kills whitefly by destroying the larvae or scales, and is commonly used to protect tomato crops from the flies, which have a record of quickly becoming resistant to chemical compounds. *Phytosiulis* is a voracious predator which is capable of quickly bringing red spider mite under control. Like whitefly, the mites have become resistant to a range of chemical compounds.

ACTIVITIES

There are many ways in which you can help make a difference in your own home, from insulating your loft to reducing consumption.

The illustration below shows some of the environmental hot spots in an average house.

A mini environmental audit

Environmental audits are a way of taking stock of our impact on the environment, so that we can devise action plans to lessen it. They are notoriously difficult activities because it is very hard to attach meaningful ecological values to different types of human activity. It is however useful to have a checklist to give you some idea of potential areas for improvement. This mini-audit is meant to be fun and not to be taken too seriously, but it might give you a few ideas. Why not get some of your friends to carry out the audit too, and compare your results? Answer each question yes, no or partly.

Energy
- Is the roof of your house insulated?
- Is your house draught proofed?
- Do you use energy efficient bulbs?

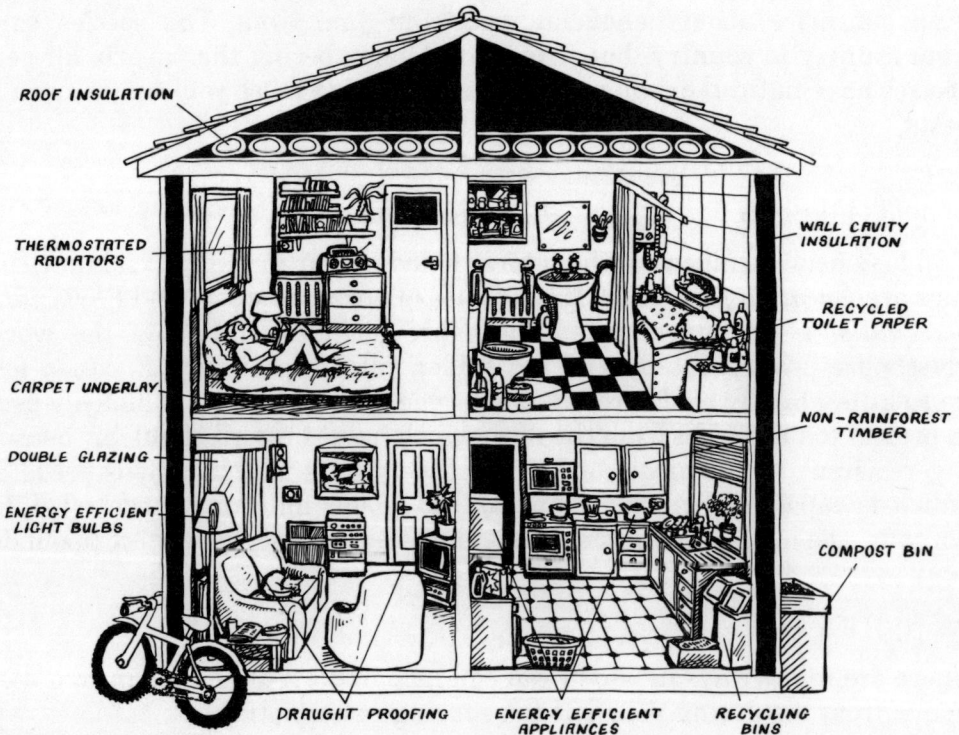

ROOF INSULATION

THERMOSTATED RADIATORS

CARPET UNDERLAY

DOUBLE GLAZING

ENERGY EFFICIENT LIGHT BULBS

WALL CAVITY INSULATION

RECYCLED TOILET PAPER

NON-RAINFOREST TIMBER

COMPOST BIN

DRAUGHT PROOFING

ENERGY EFFICIENT APPLIANCES

RECYCLING BINS

- Are your radiators controlled by thermostats?
- Is your house fitted with double glazing?
- Do your carpets have underlay?
- Do you use energy efficient goods, e.g. fridges and kettles?
- If you have air conditioning, is it thermostatically controlled?

Nature/ecology
- Do you avoid using pesticides in your garden?
- Do you encourage wildlife in your garden?
- Are you a member of a wildlife/conservation organisation?

Recycling
- Do you recycle paper?
- Do you recycle glass?
- Do you recycle cans?
- Do you recycle plastics?
- Do you make your own compost?

Transport
- Do you use public transport?
- Do you share cars/lifts?
- Do you walk/cycle where possible?
- If you have a vehicle, is it fitted with catalytic converters?

Shopping
- Do you avoid purchasing timber extracted from tropical forests?
- Do you specify recycled: writing paper? toilet paper?
- Do you reuse redundant packaging, e.g. cardboard?
- Do you reuse polythene bags?

Pollution
- Is the boiler regularly checked?
- Do you avoid burning waste?
- Is engine oil returned to local garages for recycling?
- If you have air conditioning, is it regularly serviced?

Discuss the results with your friends and brainstorm some ideas as to how you could improve your home's environmental performance. Think about which changes would best be brought about through political change, and which measures are best tackled through personal action. If you don't have a car, discuss the advantages and disadvantages of this. For each disadvantage, think of a measure or piece of legislation that could make your life easier.

Start your own nature garden

Starting a nature garden is a good way of playing an active role in the environment. What you grow in a nature garden will largely depend upon your local area. Where possible you should try to grow native species, because these will create the optimum conditions to encourage local plants and animals. One of the best examples of a successful nature garden I have come across was created at the back of a school in the United States, where an area of waste ground was used to re-establish long-grass habitat—nearly all of the natural long-grass prairie has now disappeared from the United States. By developing this area, the young people concerned saved it from being converted into a parking lot. That particular project had the advantage of having a fair amount of space on which to develop. Nature gardens can, however, be developed in quite small areas, although a smaller area will attract fewer species.

You do not need an enormous budget to start a nature garden, but what you do need is time and patience. There are a few common features that will apply to most nature gardens:

Wood piles

Rotting wood is ideal for attracting local minibeasts. It is often said that in a forest ecosystem a dead tree is worth as much as a live tree. Dead wood provides a home for insects such as beetles, which are food for local birds, and as the wood degrades a whole range of fungi species are also encouraged.

Stone piles

It might seem a little strange to put piles of stones in a nature garden, but they make good hiding places for predatory insects, lizards and slow-worms (*Anguis fragilis*). Build your stone pile in a shady area.

Soil removal

In areas where soils have become very rich through prolonged use for agriculture or gardening, a layer of topsoil often has to be removed if rarer meadow plants are to be encouraged. Highly fertile soil also allows strong weed species to dominate.

Long grass

Uncut grass can provide habitat for small mammals, and although you probably wouldn't want your nature garden covered with long grass, you can encourage diversity by leaving some of the grass uncut. The species of grass you choose is also likely to be important. Find out which species are native to your area.

Ponds

Ponds can be an enormous asset to a nature garden and help encourage a wide range of species. But if you are planning on building a pond, make certain that you have a large enough space and sufficient resources, because they are expensive to create and can be difficult to maintain.

Choice of tree

If you are growing trees, choose native species where possible, or species such as mountain ash that bear edible berries. Trees need plenty of space to grow, so make sure that you have enough room for the mature plant: trees will not thrive if they are planted too close together.

Insect-friendly plants

Some species of plant can be used to attract insects: buddleia, nettles, honey-suckle, lavender, clover and poppies will all attract butterflies, moths and bees. If you are planting a hedge, opt for plants that bear edible berries. Mixed hedges are better in most situations than single-species hedges.

Portable insect garden

If you have not got space where you live for an entire nature garden, you can always create an insect garden from largish plant boxes or tubs. Place some stones or pebbles in the base of each container for drainage. Fill with an environmentally sound compost and plant insect-attracting species of plants such as lavender, poppies and a range of sweet-smelling plants. Do not overcrowd the tubs, as most plants need plenty of room to grow. If you wish to feed your plants, a seaweed-based liquid feed promotes steady, even growth (do not use it, however, on plants that like an acid soil).

Encouraging birds in your garden

Birds are among the most loved of all wild animals, and not without reason: watching them in action can be absorbing and rewarding. These days, many birds rely on nesting sites provided either intentionally or accidentally by

human beings. If you have a garden, no matter how large or small, it is possible to encourage birds by putting up nesting boxes or feeding tables. However, helping birds successfully requires a little knowledge about the natural habitat and nesting requirements of individual species. You also need to bear in mind likely predators.

Bird table

No complicated equipment is needed to make an effective bird table. Just take a small ordinary household tray with a lip, and cut a couple of small sections away from the lip to allow for cleaning. Place the tray on top of an inverted biscuit tin and fasten both securely to a post as shown in the diagram.

The biscuit tin protects the birds from attack by predators such as cats, and stops squirrels eating the food. Any animal climbing the post will have a difficult job to get further than the tin, which effectively prevents access to the tray.

Nesting boxes

Many of the nesting boxes available in shops are built to look attractive to people and not to be user-friendly for birds. What is important is not what a box looks like, but that you understand the nesting requirements of the birds you wish to colonise your garden. A little imagination can go a long way in providing nesting sites. A large, open-ended box fastened to a high place is all that is needed for hawks and owls. Or you can hang an old kettle or saucepan from the branch of a tree, being careful to make certain that it is not too exposed and reasonably hidden from below. A hanging nesting box or one placed underneath a branch is always a good idea, because this protects nests from attack by predators. Surprisingly, a pile of old timber can also provide an ideal nesting site for many birds, as well as a source of insect food. Birds are smaller than most of their enemies, and can expertly hide their nests well within the pile. Small birds require boxes of differing dimensions, with holes of differing sizes. In order to find out the require-

ments of individual species, your best bet is to get in touch with your local ornithological society or contact an organisation such as the Royal Society for the Protection of Birds (see back of book for details).

Bats

Some people are batty about bats, while others imagine them as blood-sucking vermin. In fact, only one species, the vampire bat of Africa, actually sucks blood, and it usually attacks cattle. Most bats are harmless and even beneficial, as they eat small insects on the wing and thus help keep pest species under control. Other bats are vegetarians. In Malaysia one species of fruit bat, which lives in limestone caves, is crucial to the fertilisation of one of the country's favourite fruits, the duran, which is not often favoured by Westerners because of its very strange smell. A decline in the number of habitable caves has led to a decline in this species, but now they are carefully protected.

Due in part to their bad image bats have often been neglected, and programmes aimed at protecting them overlooked. This situation is gradually changing, and bats are now a protected species in many countries. You can play your part in protecting bats by erecting bat boxes. The effort is worthwhile: with their frenetic aerobatics, bats are fascinating creatures to watch.

Building a bat box

To build a bat box, use soft wood with no wood preservative at least 25 mm (1 inch) thick. The rough edges of the wood should be left to give the bats something to grip on to. The entrance slit of the box should be under the base of the box, at the front or back, and should be between 15 and 20 mm (½ in to ¾ in) wide. Site in an area where bats are known to feed. Place the boxes in a sheltered position as high above the ground as possible. An area beneath a tree canopy is ideal.

COLLEGE GROUNDS, SCHOOL GROUNDS AND PARKS

If you attend a school or college, why not suggest the idea of starting a nature garden and running the grounds in a more ecologically sound way? Remember that all parts of the school grounds are an ecological resource. With some careful planning, species of plant and animals can be encouraged throughout the grounds. Even if your school or college is largely covered with tarmac, a lot can be done to encourage wildlife and make the area a more pleasant environment. Throughout the world many millions of hectares of land are owned by schools and colleges, and many of these areas are ecological wastelands. If only a little was done in each, many species would be protected and diversity encouraged on quite a significant scale.

If you wish to sell the idea to teachers and principals, point out that developing a school ground as a natural resource improves the area for students as well as wildlife. The best way of taking things forward is to get together with a teacher or a group of teachers who are interested in the environment and put forward a proposal to the principal or headteacher. If you use the skills of parents, local residents and businesses, it is amazing how cheaply you can transform a school's grounds.

Encourage your school to sow an area with grasses native to your area and leave them to grow long, cutting once or maybe twice a year. Long grass is an important habitat for many species of small mammals. Native grass species will support a more diverse range of animals than non-native species. Encourage your school to plant native trees in areas around the site. Several trees grouped together in a copse not only look pleasing, but also support more species than trees planted singly.

Try to stop the use of pesticides and artificial fertilisers within the school grounds. Fertilisers are often used to promote healthy growth of grasses and to keep sports pitches looking green. However, their application also speeds up the growth of grass and therefore leads to extra cutting being necessary. Spraying weedkiller stops the development of native species of plant. If spraying is stopped, many wild species can find a home within the grounds.

If you are based on a tarmacked site, suggest that tubbed plants are added in strategic places. If you use native berry-bearing shrubs, you can attract birds as well as insects to your school. Some species of shrub, such as honeysuckle, are particularly suitable for attracting butterflies, moths and bees. You could also encourage your school to consider a school pond or wetland area.

80

5   Air Pollution

Of all types of pollution, air pollution is one of the most insidious and one of the most difficult to do anything about. It affects human health and poses a threat to the natural world. So what are its main causes and what can the individual do about it?

On an international scale, most air pollution is caused by burning fossil fuels such as oil, natural gas and coal. Although these days the thick industrial smog of the nineteenth century is no longer common in developed countries, millions of cars and lorries have taken the place of the smoky factories of the past. Many of the pollutants given off by these vehicles are poisonous even in low concentrations. What is more, this type of pollution is largely invisible and we breathe it in without even knowing. Although motor vehicles are not the only source of pollution, they are one of the most important (see below).

One way of easing the effects of pollution from motor vehicles is by using catalytic converters. These devices, which are fitted to the exhaust pipes of vehicles, contain a ceramic or metallic honeycomb coated with certain precious metals such as platinum. Contact between exhaust emissions and the honeycomb produces a chemical reaction which makes the polluting gases up to 90 per cent less harmful. Carbon monoxide is turned into carbon dioxide, and hydrocarbons are converted into carbon dioxide and water; nitrogen oxides become nitrogen. There are two types of device: two-way catalytic converters cut down carbon monoxide and hydrocarbons but not nitrogen oxides, while a three-way converter cuts down all three gases.

Unfortunately, catalytic converters are not a complete solution. The number of cars is increasing at such a rate that the beneficial effects of fitting converters will soon be negated. In addition, the devices are only effective after the engine has warmed up; before that, a car continues to pollute the atmosphere willy-nilly. And catalytic converters simply reduce the level of toxic pollutants—they do nothing to tackle the problem of global warming caused by exhaust emissions.

With so many people reliant on motor cars, cutting their use is not going to be easy. Public transport systems throughout the developed world are just not adequate, at present, to cope with the volume of goods and passengers now being conveyed by private transport. Car ownership itself has become synonymous with development, so many developing countries are increasing their reliance on motor vehicles. Perhaps a complete solution to this problem will only be found when oil stocks become depleted and people are forced to look for alternatives.

Photochemical smog

Photochemical smog is caused when certain oxides of nitrogen and hydrocarbons come together in strong sunlight, when a series of chemical reactions forms the poisonous gas ozone. Motor vehicles are a major cause of this type of smog.

MYTH-BUSTERS

Ozone up there—ozone down here

There is more confusion about ozone pollution than any other environmental problem. In the upper atmosphere ozone is useful, forming a protective barrier to the sun's harmful ultraviolet rays. However, at ground level ozone is a serious pollutant. So ozone depletion and ozone pollution are two totally different issues.

LOW-LEVEL OZONE

While concentrations of sulphur dioxide are decreasing in many industrial countries, the levels of low-level ozone seem to be rising, and this form of pollution is becoming a serious environmental problem. As a pollutant, ozone is particularly harmful: it can aggravate breathing difficulties and childhood asthma even at low concentrations. At high concentrations, ozone can cause serious damage to the lungs and can harm the immune system; it can also cause coughing and choking, particularly in those taking vigorous exercise, such as joggers. Ozone also damages plants, especially when mixed with other gases such as sulphur dioxide. A growing body of evidence

suggests that ozone may have some role in areas of forests dying off: controlled experiments have shown that it can damage trees. Concentrations of low-level ozone are often particularly high in photochemical smog.

Traffic pollution

From London to Los Angeles, from New York to New Delhi, air pollution is choking our cities. In 1989, according to the Organisation for Economic Cooperation and Development (OECD), motor vehicles caused 75 per cent of carbon monoxide pollution, 48 per cent of pollution from nitrogen oxides, and 13 per cent of hydrocarbons in member countries. In cities, the proportion of pollution caused by motor vehicles is likely to be even higher.

In the United States the worst air pollution is found in Los Angeles. The Greater Los Angeles basin has 8 million cars spewing 1,246 tonnes of noxious pollutants into its atmosphere every day, often leading to a photochemical haze hanging over the city—Los Angeles smog. In 1990, the California Air Resources Board (CARB) took action, demanding that, by 1998, 2 per cent of all new cars sold in the state by the big manufacturers should have no exhaust emissions. That number should rise to 5 per cent in 2001, and 10 per cent by 2003, but California still has a long way to go to meet nationally agreed air-quality targets. But, as a result of these targets, motor companies such as Ford are now investigating the viability of commercially producing electrically powered cars.

Action on ozone

If you live in an area affected by photochemical smog, contact your local authority and find out what they are doing to tackle low-level ozone. During a particularly hot and still period in 1994, some German authorities advised motorists to stay at home.

If you or your parents have a car, consider having it fitted with a catalytic converter. This helps to reduce the levels of polluting gases that it produces.

In some countries, air-quality warnings are given on television broadcasts, including weather forecasts in the UK. If you suffer from breathing difficulties, take extra care during periods of photochemical smog.

Write to your national political representative and find out what is being done on a national level to tackle the problem of low-level ozone.

GLOBAL WARMING

Perhaps more misleading information has been written about global warming than about any other subject covered in this book. The earth's climate is so complex and unpredictable that no one really knows what the long-term effects of global warming will be. All the same, its causes are fairly well known.

The main cause of global warming—I prefer to call it global climate change, as not everywhere will necessarily warm up—is the mass emissions of gases into the atmosphere from the burning of fossil fuel. Since almost all activity in industrialised society, such as transport and industrial production, relies on burning fossil fuels, it is difficult to see how we can stop the process of global warming without enormous international effort. As countries become more developed so they use more fossil fuels, so the global burning of fossil fuels continues to increase.

The gases that cause global warming are known as greenhouse gases, because they reflect long-wave radiation emitted from the earth's surface, and so warm the earth by helping to retain heat, rather like the glass in a greenhouse. The most important is carbon dioxide or CO_2, but others include water vapour, methane, nitrogen oxides and CFCs. To some extent, these gases are essential to our atmosphere. If they were all removed, the earth would be a frightening 30°C cooler than it is now, and life as we know it could not exist. The problem we face now, however, is that so many greenhouse gases are being emitted that the atmosphere's natural self-regulatory mechanisms cannot cope with them. The result is likely to be a net increase in global temperatures: I say likely, because certainty is lacking in all scientific studies dealing with this subject.

Climate scientists use powerful computers to try to predict the effect on the world's climate. While this can give a rough guide, exact predictions are impossible because so many different factors are at play. Sunspot activity, for example, also affects the earth's climate, as do other equally unquantifiable things. The scientists' best guess at the moment is that global temperatures will increase by around 3°C over the next 50 years, but not everyone agrees with this figure.

The best rule to apply in cases like this is called the precautionary principle—if in doubt, play safe. Reducing our influence on the global climate is likely to be a slow process because the world's industrial activity cannot just stop, and developing alternatives to fossil fuels will undoubtedly take time. That means that we need to prioritise methods of reducing CO_2 emissions to achieve the greatest effect in the shortest time. It also means that people will need to be patient. Slowing global climate change will not happen overnight. Even if we stopped producing CO_2 today, it would be a number of years before its levels began to show significant decline. One good candidate for early improvement is the production of electricity, which unit for unit is far more wasteful of fuel than other forms of energy.

MYTH-BUSTERS

Global warming will make plants grow better

It has been speculated that higher temperatures, together with increased levels of CO_2, which is a plant nutrient, will lead to increased growth rates. But since no one is certain of the exact effects of global climate change, this is an unsafe assumption. A rise of a couple of degrees, together with drier summers, could prove devastating for grain farmers in the American Midwest, for example, and thus catastrophic for world food supplies. This is an assumption too, but should we be gambling with our climate?

If the ice in the Arctic Ocean melts, sea levels will rise

Sea-level rise could be caused by the expansion of water in the earth's oceans and the melting of glaciers and land-based ice. This could cause flooding, and is a serious threat for low-lying islands such as the Maldives. However, the melting of sea-based ice alone would have no effect. To prove this, try floating an ice cube in a tumbler of water—measure the water level before and after the ice has melted. A far greater threat is the melting of land-based ice, which could release huge quantities of methane stored beneath permafrost. Methane is a powerful greenhouse gas, so the melting of this ice would itself add to global warming.

Take action on global warming

Many governments are now seeking to stabilise the emissions of greenhouse gases. The European Community, for example, has set a target of reducing greenhouse gases to 1990 levels by the year 2000 (see Chapter 7). This may be a step in the right direction but it is hardly enough, particularly if one bears in mind that emissions are likely to rise globally. Some countries, such as Denmark, have been a lot bolder in their approach.

The Danish approach

In April 1990 the Danish Government put forward an adventurous action plan called *Energy 2000: a plan for sustainable development*. The plan set ambitious targets for a total reduction in CO_2 emissions of 20 per cent by the year 2000, though this date has since been revised to 2005. These targets were based on a detailed assessment of the Danish economy, together with an assessment of savings that could be made through a range of activities. The plan put forward a range of practical proposals including:

- encouraging energy efficiency
- developing district heating schemes
- the development of new technology (including wind power and biomass)
- energy labelling of all electrical appliances
- energy taxes
- incentives for industries embarking on energy efficiency programmes

The plan also proposed the increased use of natural gas for generating electricity as an interim measure to reduce the output of sulphur dioxide. These measures taken together, the plan argued, were important to Denmark economically. 'Failure to act now,' the report concluded, 'will as time marches on make it more and more difficult and costly to achieve the same results.' Since then Denmark has reviewed the initiative, and a follow-up report published in November 1993 announced some additional energy-efficiency measures.

Other countries could learn a lot from Denmark's example. Setting international targets such as these would be a significant first step in tackling global warming. While this may take a few years to bring about, continued lobbying of politicians and awareness-raising will help. You could write to your local authority asking them what is being done locally to conserve energy or highlighting energy wastage, for example in schools and colleges. Point out the targets set by Denmark, and the advantages of energy efficiency programmes. Why not ask your school or college to put on a special global warming day, to help raise awareness of the issues? On a personal level, conserving energy will make a difference, no matter how small.

Acid rain

Acid pollution continues to pose a threat to lakes and forests throughout the world, despite attempts by many countries to introduce cleaner technologies. Technically, acid rain is just what it says—acidified rainwater. There are, however, several other forms of acid pollution, including acid fog, mist and snow. Acid rain is a secondary pollutant which forms when primary pollutants such as sulphur dioxide and nitrogen oxide react with water vapour in the atmosphere. Many of these polluting gases come from coal-fired power stations, although motorised transport is an increasing source of nitrogen oxides. Airborne pollution is no respector of international boundaries: acid rain from parts of the USA affects areas of Canada, for example, and acid pollution from Britain affects lakes in Sweden. This is because once the polluting substances get into the atmosphere they can be blown considerable distances by the wind before they fall as rain.

Among the worst-affected forests in Europe are those in Poland, where considerable damage has been caused by the burning of high-sulphur coal by Polish industry. Lakes in Canada and Sweden have also been badly affected. Although the introduction of cleaner technology has helped take a little of the heat out of the debate on acid rain, levels of acid pollution remain a serious international concern. Not only does acid rain threaten our wildlife habitats; it also threatens many historic buildings. Among the famous monuments affected by air pollution are the Taj Mahal in India and St Paul's Cathedral in London.

Protecting the Taj Mahal

In August 1993 the Indian Supreme Court shut down more than 200 factories in order to protect the Taj Mahal from the effects of air pollution. This unique seventeenth-century white marble monument was yellowing due to the effects of smoke-belching factories. The Indian authorities, recognising the importance of the monument as a tourist attraction, closed down factories which failed to cut their pollution levels. This is the type of tough action necessary if the damage caused by acid rain is to be halted. In October

1993 the court also moved to close down factories polluting the River Ganges which flows for 2,400 kilometres from the Himalayas and is the main source of water for many families. More than 190 industries were ordered to close immediately, most of them being tanneries or distilleries.

Take action on acid pollution

Normal rainfall has a pH value of between 4.5 and 5.5, depending on where you live. If rainfall in your area has a pH of below 4.5 then it is likely that you suffer from acid rain. You can try monitoring levels of pollution by collecting rainwater in a clean plastic beaker through a funnel. Measure the pH value of the rain after every period of rainfall using either litmus paper or pH indicator solution. Keep a note of the values. It is interesting to compare the results from several areas. If you find your rain is more acidic than it should be, send your results to your MP or member of Congress, highlighting the level of pollution and enquiring about national strategy on reducing acid pollution. Also, find out more about the work of national environmental organisations working on the issue of acid rain.

Ozone depletion

Very few people had heard of the ozone layer before 1985 when scientists working in the Antarctic discovered a 'hole' in the upper atmosphere—it is actually an area where ozone is considerably thinner than normal. The idea of an ozone layer is itself a little misleading because ozone is spread over a considerable belt in the upper atmosphere, or stratosphere, between ten and 50 kilometres (six and 30 miles) above sea level, but concentrated at the upper level in the area called 'the ozone layer'. During the Antarctic winter the hole is at its largest, covering an area the size of the United States. The exact causes of the Antarctic ozone hole are still not fully understood, but it soon became clear that pollution contributes to the destruction of ozone or ozone depletion.

Ozone depletion can have serious consequences because the ozone layer absorbs 99 per cent of the ultraviolet (UV) part of the sun's rays, preventing them reaching the Earth. These rays are damaging to all life, and have been linked with skin cancer. The most damaging rays are known as ultraviolet B (UVB).

How does ozone depletion take place?

In 1974, two American scientists discovered that chlorofluorocarbons or CFCs could destroy ozone. Before that discovery, CFCs had been considered an ideal chemical because they are nonflammable and nontoxic. Due to their stable nature, CFC molecules remain in the atmosphere for many years. Eventually they work their way up to the stratosphere, where they are broken apart by rays of ultraviolet light. As they break up, they release chlorine atoms which destroy ozone through a catalytic reaction. One CFC molecule can destroy up to 10,000 ozone molecules.

In the Antarctic the problem is particularly bad during the winter, when spiralling air movements combine with very low temperatures to accelerate ozone depletion. The ozone hole appears when concentrations of chlorine reach 1.5–2.00 parts per billion (ppb).

It is a testimony to the complexity of environmental issues that to this day scientists do not fully agree on the degree to which synthetic chemicals cause ozone holes. Natural phenomena certainly play a role, and some scientists even argue that the holes are entirely natural. Indeed, there are significant natural sources of atmospheric chlorine, including volcanic eruptions. But the evidence suggests that synthetic chemicals, including CFCs, do deplete ozone, some, such as halons, because of the release of bromide rather than chlorine, so removing them from the environment remains essential.

The table below lists some of the most common ozone-depleting chemicals.

Chemical	Use
CFCs (Chlorofluorocarbons)	Fridge and air-conditioning coolant; insulation for buildings; cleaner for electrical components
HCFCs (Hydrochlorofluorocarbons)	Fridge coolant; insulative foam; solvents; some aerosols
Methyl chloroform	Metal cleaning; some adhesives; electronic cleaning
Carbon tetrachloride	Chemical processes such as the production of CFCs
Halons	Fire extinguishers

Health effects

Ultraviolet light is not necessarily bad for the human body. In low doses it helps in the formation of vitamin D in the skin. The problem arises when the dose of UV becomes too great. It is thought, for example, that a decrease of only 1 per cent of tropospheric ozone could lead to a 3 per cent rise in the number of skin cancers. Apart from cancer, UV light can also cause cataracts, snow-blindness, sunburn and ageing of the skin; in addition, UV light can lower the resistance of the skin, making tumours more likely. But increases in UV light will not only affect humans, but also animals, plants and synthetic materials.

Hope for the future

If we stop using ozone-depleting chemicals then the ozone hole can recover, given time. This is because ozone is formed naturally in the upper atmosphere. But the need for urgent action remains strong, so ozone depletion is not a dead issue. Due to the relatively long life of ozone-depleting chemicals, it could be that the ozone layer will take a century or more to repair itself.

In 1987 the Montreal Protocol was signed by many of the world's leading industrial nations. This treaty called for a 50 per cent reduction in the production of CFCs by 1998. In June 1990 the protocol was revised and it was agreed to phase out ozone-depleting chemicals by the year 2000. This was very good news and a positive result for many environmental groups which had been campaigning on the issue. But it is likely that ozone-depleting chemicals will continue to be used in many developing nations which cannot afford the alternatives. It is up to the developed nations to help these countries by technological transfer programmes, which provide the necessary expertise and technology. Ozone-depleting chemicals are still being produced, and much remains to be done. Perhaps what is most important is that we learn the lessons that ozone depletion has to teach us.

The lessons of ozone depletion

Synthesised chemicals released into the atmosphere can have repercussions very far from the site of release. New chemicals should therefore be extensively tested before being commercially marketed. Pollution itself is often insidious: its effects are not always easy to recognise and even when they are, it is not always easy to prove that a particular agent is to blame. Recycling and care when handling toxic chemicals should always be a top priority.

90

Take action

Encourage your parents, teachers, lecturers to:

- Recycle CFC from old refrigerators before they are scrapped. Immediately repair any refrigerators showing signs of leaking coolants.
- Avoid purchasing halon fire extinguishers
- Avoid air conditioning in cars and houses if at all possible. Light-coloured cars with white interiors stay cooler than darker ones.
- Avoid installing air conditioning to keep buildings cool in summer. Various alternative measures can be used, including coating the roof with light-coloured sealant or planting trees at the sunny side of the building. Fan-cooling systems are a better way to keep cool and are far less environmentally damaging. If you do have air conditioning, make certain that it is regularly serviced.
- Check all products before purchase to avoid ozone-damaging chemicals.
- Write to one or two electronics companies and ask them what their policy is on CFCs and other ozone-depleting chemicals. Some companies have stopped using CFCs in the production of computer chips, but others continue to use ozone-depleting substances. Ask whether the company has an environmental policy and if so whether you can have a copy.
- Find out from an environmental group the names of ozone-depleting chemicals produced in your country. Write to the manufacturers and ask them what they are doing to research alternatives and phase out production.

ACTIVITIES

Survey of air pollution

One way to find out the main source of air pollution in your area is by doing a simple particulate survey. The method given here will give you a rough idea of the amount of particulate pollution locally.

Use holly, laurel or any evergreen leaf, but use the same species of plant throughout the experiment. Select leaves that are one year old—they will be a darker colour. If you look at the stems, these leaves will be behind the first set of scars on the darker wood (see diagram overleaf).

Stick some strips of adhesive tape onto two or three leaves, and press them down lightly. Take samples from different sides of your plant. Immediately remove the strips of tape, taking care not to remove the surface of the leaf. Stick the tape onto your record sheets.

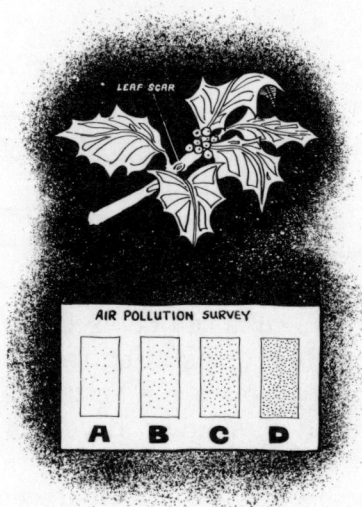

Use a different record sheet for each location. You will need to take quite a number of different samples if you are going to get a range of results. For a really interesting set of results, you should choose your locations carefully. Take areas of different land use such as main trunk roads, side roads, parkland, industrial areas, residential areas, rural areas and town centres. To cover a large area it is worth looking at a map and dividing your area of study among a group of friends and classmates.

White paper

You can also use sheets of white paper to pick up particulates. You should conduct this experiment in two different locations, one which you suspect to be polluted and another which you suspect to be clean. Place one strip of paper a week in a dry place out of direct sunlight. After eight weeks, collect the pieces of paper and have a look at them. All paper fades after a while, but paper stained by particulates will look darker and sootier than paper placed in an unpolluted site. This test will show up particulate pollutants, but will tell you nothing about invisible air pollution. For that you will need to conduct another type of test such as the lichen survey below. It is also possible to buy indicator kits, which will give you readings for individual gases.

Lichen survey

Another way of surveying air pollution is through what is known as indicator species. Indicator species are types of plant, animal or fungus that are particularly vulnerable to pollution. In the case of air pollution, lichen can be used as indicators since some species are far more tolerant of pollution than others. Some lichens are killed by very small amounts of polluting gases such as sulphur dioxide. Lichens are very sensitive to heavy metals such as lead. These types of lichen are therefore not usually found by roads because of the lead used in some petrol.

Lichens are common in most countries since they develop from spores which are easily blown from place to place. The top half of the lichen is a fungus, while the base is made up of algae. These two separate organisms live in perfect harmony to make what is in effect a single organism, one of many examples found in nature of two organisms working for mutual benefit, a process known as a symbiotic relationship.

Conducting your survey

For the purpose of this survey, it is useful to imagine your country being divided into different zones, ranging from highly polluted to extremely clean. The table below gives a rough guide, but figures will vary from country to country.

Zone 0—lichen desert	0–2 species
Zone 1—badly polluted	3–4 species
Zone 2—fairly polluted	5–6 species
Zone 3—moderate	7–8 species
Zone 4—fairly clean	9–10 species
Zone 5—clean	10–11 species
Zone 6—excellent	12 and more species

Lichens grow on trees, stones or artificial surfaces; however, for the purpose of this survey, look at lichens on only one surface, ideally on trees. This is because the type of surface has an effect on how tolerant the lichen is to pollution.

Generally, the more types of species of lichen that you find in an area, the less polluted the air is, but finding a lot of one species does not necessarily mean that the air is clean. Some species of lichen are difficult to identify, so you will need a book illustrating lichens to be able to identify them.

93

Further action

Finding out about pollution is fascinating, but you might want to go further and do something to change the situation. Personal action such as cycling, using public transport or sharing transport is a start, but really to tackle the problems some local and national legislation is likely to be necessary. There is no reason why young people should not be involved in the process of bringing about political change. Under the Earth Summit agreement at Rio de Janeiro in Brazil, governments agreed to take account of what young people had to say about what is, after all, their future. Pressure from young people helps keep issues on the agenda, especially as often many of those who are not already voters will be by the time an election comes round. Air pollution and climate change are two of the most difficult issues to get governments to move on, because our economies rely to such an extent on fossil fuels and the automobile, so continuing pressure does help.

6   Our Seas and Rivers

WATER POLLUTION

For many people water has something mystical about it—it represents purity. In ancient times, rivers and lakes assumed spiritual significance and were associated with gods and nymphs. A spring not only represented purity, but was a source of life and vital water to grow crops. Today, our seas and rivers are a source of rich food which sustains many human communities. Yet only a tiny percentage of the earth's water is suitable for use by human beings for drinking and irrigation. As much as 97 per cent is in oceans and seas, and much of the remaining water is held in polar icecaps. People living in arid parts of the world can immediately understand the precious nature of water, but many of us simply take water for granted as being available at the turn of a tap. Perhaps we need to recapture some of our ancient wonder and treat our water supplies with more respect. Using water sensibly and protecting it from careless pollution is something that we can all take a part in.

The problems

The unfortunate fact seems to be that wherever water is found, it ends up getting polluted. Our seas, rivers and lakes are all affected in one way or another. Our careless use of water today could cause problems for years or even generations ahead. This cycle of water pollution has meant that polluting substances have reached some of the most remote ecosystems on earth. One of the most dramatic examples of this is provided by the beluga whale. This rare and unique mammal is the only freshwater whale in the

95

world. In the St Lawrence river in Canada, beluga whales have become so toxic as a result of water pollution that under Canadian law their bodies have to be disposed of as toxic waste. Industrial pollutants have got into the water and worked their way through the food chain, and the whales have become the unfortunate victims of human carelessness.

Reducing the level of pollution in our rivers, lakes and seas is an urgent priority, not just for animals such as the beluga whale, but for all life on earth, including humans. In many developing nations, having clean water supplies can mean the difference between life and death.

The drinking water crisis

In sub-Saharan Africa, drinking-water supply and sanitation are among the worst in the world, according to the World Health Organisation. In 1990 nearly 500 million people were living in sub-Saharan Africa: 265 million of these lacked safe drinking water, and 344 million lived without adequate sanitation facilities. Population growth has largely offset the progress achieved during recent decades: in some of the worst drought-affected countries, the amount of renewable fresh water per person has dropped by more than 65 per cent in the last 40 years. At this rate, according to the World Health Organisation, supply per person will be a mere 15 per cent of the 1955 value by 2025. During 1993, a total of 72,500 cholera cases were recorded in sub-Saharan Africa, approximately 3 per cent of them being fatal. In Latin America, more than 200,000 cases were recorded over the same period, with a death rate of 1 per cent.

A depleted resource

The giant Aral Sea, between Kazakhstan and Uzbekistan in the former Soviet Union, has for centuries provided people with a source of fresh water. Today, however, due largely to less water entering the lake from its river sources, the lake is less than half the size it was 25 years ago. In the United States, the vast underground water supply of the great plains has been depleted to such an extent that the water table is falling by around a metre a year in eight states. During the early 1990s a number of streams in the United Kingdom dried up, despite the country's relatively wet climate, largely as the result of the over-extraction of water, which caused a fall in the level of ground water.

Water, like any other resource, should be used with care if we are to preserve supplies. Adults require just two litres (four pints) of water per day to meet their biological needs, but an average household in the developed world uses around 200 litres (50 gallons) per person per day. Modern washing machines use around 150 litres (40 gallons) per wash on a normal cycle. But even more water is used in manufacturing processes. For example, it requires 350 litres (90 gallons) of water to make just one litre (two pints) of beer, and huge amounts are used in food production.

THE CAUSES

Water becomes polluted in many ways. Some of the more obvious sources of water pollution include human sewage, industrial wastes and agricultural wastes, chemicals and fertilisers. However, water also becomes polluted as a result of acid rain which can drift hundreds of miles, affecting streams and lakes far from its source.

Action against pollution – the Mackenzie River

The Mackenzie River is located in the far north of Canada, in the Northwest Territories, with a watershed encompassing parts of the Yukon, British Columbia, Alberta, Saskatchewan and the Northwest Territories. The river itself flows north into the Arctic Ocean, in a delta where little pollution might be expected due to sparse population and a low level of industrial development. But even here, concern over water pollution has been expressed by local fishermen. In the settlement of Fort Good Hope, fish have

97

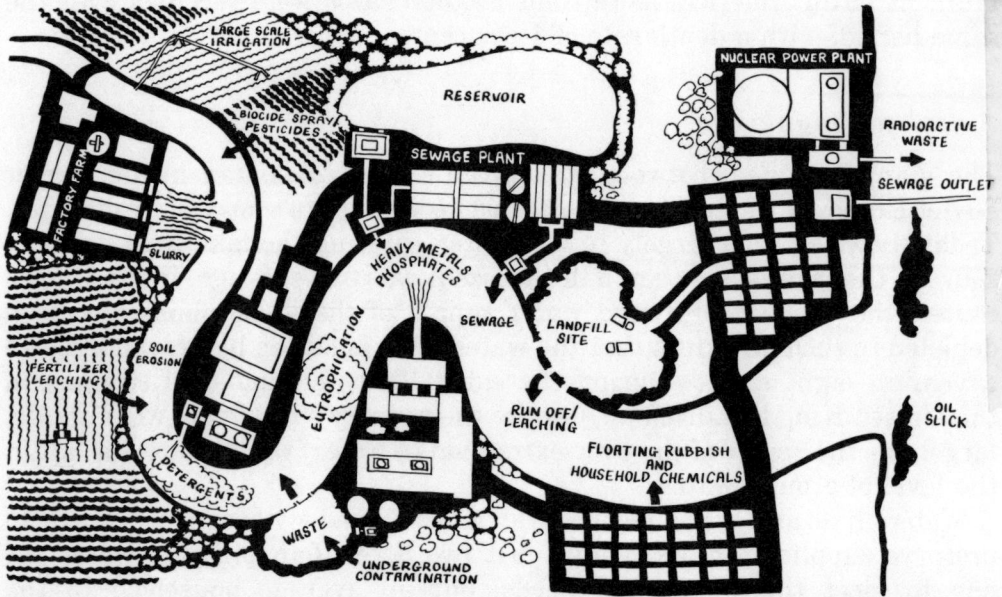

been caught with abnormally large livers, which local people believe are the result of hydrocarbons in the water. The problem for the fishermen is that the settlement is downstream from the Mackenzie's huge drainage basin, which contains a number of industrial developments, including large paper mills in northern Alberta.

Efforts to preserve the ecology of the Mackenzie river basin have involved the jurisdictions of five territories, together with two federal departments (Environment Canada and DIAND), which are currently in the process of negotiating a trans-boundary water agreement for the entire basin. Various community-based programmes have concentrated on environmental clean-ups and schemes allowing fishermen to bring in any fish showing signs of abnormality. Together, these schemes should help to protect a unique area of wilderness in northern Canada.

Pollution from sewage

One of the most serious causes of water pollution is treated and untreated sewage discharged into our rivers and seas. Although waste discharged into rivers is often treated, it is difficult to remove all the phosphates and heavy metals. Many water suppliers have managed to improve the quality of sewage treatment, but in many countries this type of pollution remains a severe problem. Much of the sewage discharged to the sea is untreated.

The Mediterranean Sea

The coastal areas of the Mediterranean are places of stupendous beauty. Some of the world's first civilised societies took root around this large sea, which divides Europe from North Africa. It provides a dream venue for the millions of holiday-makers who seek to relax on one of the many sandy beaches or mysterious islands, against the perfect backdrop of a seemingly pure and peaceful blue sea. Unfortunately, this idyllic, unpolluted image is far from the truth. The Mediterranean is one of the most polluted seas on earth, and if anything the pressures it faces are getting ever greater. Although it makes up only one per cent of all the world's ocean area, the Mediterranean has to cope with almost 50 per cent of all marine pollution.

The main pollutants are industrial wastes and sewage, around 80 per cent of which is poured into the sea untreated. The industrial wastes emanate from the industrial areas of the Mediterranean; pollution from the nations surrounding the Black Sea also finds its way into the Mediterranean through the Bosphorous. One of the sea's particular problems is that it has a very poor capacity for self-cleansing, being almost entirely landlocked with only the narrow Straits of Gibraltar connecting it to the Atlantic. In this relatively closed system, pollutants end up trapped within the confines of the sea itself. These problems have been added to by the huge number of tourists visiting the area, which at least doubles the population during the summer months. The United Nations has estimated that by 2025 up to 760 million people could be holidaying in the Mediterranean, with a resident population of around 150 million.

Once in the sea the sewage degrades, depriving the water of oxygen and spawning huge blooms of poisonous algae. The threat posed by these blooms has led the authorities in Italy's Gulf of Genoa to construct an offshore barrier 35 kilometres (22 miles) wide to prevent the slime from reaching the beach. But this exercise has not been accompanied by efforts to tackle the underlying problems of sewage and industrial pollution. Many species such as the Mediterranean monk seal are under severe threat from the high levels of pollution and the disturbance caused by tourists.

Various attempts have been made to clean up the Mediterranean, perhaps the best known of which was the Mediterranean Action Plan initiated by the United Nations in 1975. This sought to stop the dumping of toxic materials at sea and to limit the amount of toxic wastes entering the sea from land-based sources. The plan involved 16 Mediterranean countries, but has had only very limited success. Far more still needs to be done. It seems ironic that this area—with all its myths, legends and mysteries, and which epitomises the transition of the human species from simple village-based

99

societies to a fully blown civilisation—should itself suffer so greatly as a result of our modern life style.

Oily waters—the Exxon Valdez

The most publicised cases of pollution at sea are the massive, accidental spills from oil tankers. In 1989 an oil tanker, the *Exxon Valdez*, spilled around 50 million litres (12 million gallons) of crude oil into the Gulf of Alaska after it ran into reef pinnacles in Prince William Sound. The devastating oil spill affected over 2,000 kilometres (1,250 miles) of unspoiled Alaskan coast. The resulting clean-up involved thousands of people and cost in the order of a billion dollars. Many fish such as salmon, sea birds, and mammals such as sea otters and seals were killed: estimates total millions of fish, 300,000 sea birds, 950 sea otters and 150 bald eagles, but nobody knows the full total. Without a doubt, the *Exxon Valdez* disaster was the US's worst ever oil spill.

Although major spills such as this one are devastating, slicks caused by washing out waste oil from tankers and diesel-powered ships cause most oil pollution at sea. The success of Greenpeace in persuading the oil company Shell to reconsider its decision to dump an oil platform at sea in 1995 shows that even the largest companies will bow to international pressure.

Pollution from industrial wastes

A wide range of manufacturing processes causes water pollution. Particularly damaging are pollutants such as cadmium, mercury compounds and heavy metals, which can cause damage to living systems even at very low levels. Cadmium is used particularly in the metal-plating industry and is a waste product of detergent manufacture. Industrial pesticides such as moth-proofing agents used in the textile industry can also cause severe pollution problems, as can oils, solvents and effluents from the food-processing industry. Some pollutants get into groundwater, where they can persist over very long periods. Many countries have brought in legislation to try to protect their rivers and streams from industrial waste, but despite this many of our rivers contain dangerously high levels of polluting agents. In many developing countries, where pollution controls are either not so strict or nonexistent, the threats posed by water pollution are even greater.

Agricultural pollution

Artificial fertilisers are used by farmers throughout the world. Fertiliser varies in its composition, but most is composed of three substances—nitrogen, phosphorus and potassium, usually known by their chemical symbols of N, P and K—which provide farmers with an easy way to boost yields. The nitrogen components of agricultural fertiliser are highly soluble and are easily leached from the soil by rainwater to end up in rivers, lakes or groundwater. Chemical compounds from agricultural sprays also pose a threat to our fresh water, and some are extremely toxic. Some pesticides enter water due to leaching, others from drift during spraying.

In the developing world many toxic substances banned in developed nations are still freely available. In April 1993 the World Health Organisation expressed concern about the increase in pesticide poisoning, particularly in developing nations. Often a lack of hygiene, information or adequate controls has created unsafe working conditions. These conditions combine to put agricultural workers at risk.

In addition to the direct risk, spills into rivers and streams may often go unnoticed, with the result that toxic substances damage wildlife and may end up in the human food chain. The best way to stop these incidents is to stop the toxic substances concerned entering the environment in the first place.

Farm effluents

Farm effluents such as slurry and liquids seeping from silage—fermented grass—can rapidly deoxygenate water, killing fish and other aquatic life forms. It has been estimated that seepage from silage can be 200 times more harmful than raw human sewage. This type of pollution is particularly associated with intensive livestock farming, which can produce huge amounts of slurry that is difficult for farmers to dispose of (see Chapter 4).

Nutrient enrichment

Nutrient enrichment is a problem that occurs due to plant nutrients seeping into rivers, lakes or seas. This can bring about a change known as eutrophication. What happens is that the plant nutrients cause microscopic algae to grow faster, which in turn can lead to a lack of oxygen in the water. This is a particular problem at the approach of winter, when large algal blooms die off. Their decomposition removes oxygen from the water, which can kill fish and other freshwater organisms. In extreme cases, the water can be turned into a foul-smelling 'pea soup'.

101

The main nutrient that causes eutrophication is phosphate, which enters waterways from sewage, industrial processes and intensive agriculture. With modern treatment techniques this phosphate can be removed, and many water companies are now upgrading their treatment works to tackle the problem. The work of pressure groups has helped to bring about this change, which is why independent environmental groups are so important. In Britain, a national body called the NRA (National Rivers Authority) now tests and monitors the levels of pollution in streams and fresh water, and over time this work should help to improve water quality. However, a lot more still needs to be done to stop pollutants reaching our rivers and lakes. The setting of high standards for industry and water companies is only the first part of this process. It is also important to stop poisonous chemicals being poured down drains or leaking into groundwater from toxic tips. Perhaps most of all, we should respect our rivers and lakes as the living ecosystems they are.

Groundwater pollution

The pollution of groundwater from nitrates in agricultural fertilisers, solvents and toxic leachate from landfill sites is an invisible and very serious form of pollution. Groundwater is an important source of drinking water, so it is vital that we keep it pollution free. Pollutants in groundwater are very difficult to get rid of and very persistent, as the experiment at the end of the chapter demonstrates. Groundwater pollution is a growing international problem.

Luckily we have become a lot more aware of the problem, with the result that there is now far greater scrutiny of potential hazards. But groundwater pollution is likely to continue until people realise that toxic substances dumped in holes in the ground or tipped on the soil don't simply disappear.

In New York and in Birmingham in the UK, solvents and trichloroethane from the electronics industry have polluted groundwater. In the areas around the Great Lakes in Canada concern over groundwater over-extraction and pollution led to the launch in 1990 of an initiative by the Great Lakes Commission to promote the informed use, management and protection of groundwater resources. An education programme was also launched, aimed at informing young people and the general public about groundwater issues. Working with local companies, schools and voluntary groups, this initiative has helped to raise awareness and protect these valuable resources for the future.

Case study: The problem with sewage

Many countries still dump sewage sludge at sea, place it in landfill sites or incinerate it. The reason these measures are necessary is that most sewage in the industrial world contains heavy metals, which make the sewage highly toxic. Where human sewage is kept apart from industrial waste it is possible to use the resulting sludge to fertilise land. Calcutta in India has no sewage treatment works: instead, most human sewage is channelled through a series of drains into shallow lakes on the edge of the city. Here the sewage fertilises algae and plants such as watercress and water hyacinth, which in turn provide food for fish such as carp. The whole system is organised by local fishermen. So in two easy stages human waste is transformed into a valuable source of food. While this example may seem a little extreme, it represents a sustainable method of farming fish. Using plants to treat sewage has been developed in various schemes in the industrialised world too, including schemes in the United States such as a project in Arcata, that has developed wetlands for treatment of the municipal sewage.

WETLAND ECOSYSTEMS

Wetland ecosystems are among the most delicate and most threatened habitats on earth. Many are located on estuaries or along heavily populated coastlines, close to areas of industrial activity. Others are adjacent to rich agricultural areas, and are at threat from both pollution and drainage schemes. There have been many excellent schemes to protect wetland habitats. Often protecting a wetland site relies on co-operation between a number of individuals, groups and companies.

Conservation of McCarley's Swamp

McCarley's Swamp, located just north of Ludlow in western Australia, is an important site housing one of the region's largest breeding colonies of two birds, the great egret and the straw-necked ibis. The swamp suffers from water pollution from both eutrophication, partly caused by bird droppings, and seepage from local mining sites. The site is privately owned, but the landowner is sympathetic to wetland conservation, and the mining company adjacent to the site has helped in renovation work aimed at reducing the impact of mining activities. This work has consisted of some revegetation, and the removal of excess water which had resulted from the mining.

If you live in an area near wetlands, why not find out if there are any

103

conservation schemes you could be involved in? Discover what species live in the area and any threats to the environment.

Take action

Why not write to some paper and detergent manufacturers asking them what they are doing to reduce water pollution resulting from the manufacturing of their product? Ask specifically whether the company carries out pollution monitoring in local rivers or streams, and if so whether you can have the results of these tests. If you know of a factory near you that you believe to be causing pollution, write asking the same questions, and point out that the planned replacement of old equipment makes sense and is far better than waiting for legislation to force replacement. Some national bodies such as the NRA hold records of water quality. It is possible to get hold of these and compare the water quality upstream from a sewage works or factory and downstream. If you actually manage to get two sets of statistics, then you can match them up to see if they tally. If not, get back to the business concerned showing your results and ask if they can account for the disparity. Some businesses are actually willing to get together with local groups to solve pollution problems; others are willing to send environmental managers to give talks at schools or colleges.

THERE ARE ALWAYS MORE FISH IN THE SEA

The earth's seas and oceans seem an endless resource, making up two-thirds of the area of our planet. At once forbidding and barren and rich and diverse, it is little wonder that they are places of myths and legends.

Very little is known about many marine ecologies, which are among the most complex ecosystems on earth. With life in places penetrating nearly five kilometres (three miles) below the surface, we will probably never discover all the life forms inhabiting this strange world. Moves to declare the Antarctic and parts of the South Seas a global sanctuary have been very welcome, as have international attempts to prevent overfishing and to ban whaling. These moves represent undeniable progress. They are what makes fighting for the environment worthwhile. But we still have a long way to go to persuade many countries to practise sustainable fishing methods, and to protect large marine mammals such as dolphins and other cetaceans.

Overfishing itself is as much a threat to human communities as it is to marine species. Particularly in the developing world, many communities rely on fish stocks which are now becoming dangerously depleted.

104

Throughout the world, fishermen have harvested the oceans for thousands of years without apparent ill effect—so what happened?

One of the problems that gave rise to overfishing on a massive scale is that there was never any recognised ownership for the natural resources of the ocean. This, together with modern fishing technology, meant that any nation with a fishing fleet could go out and harvest fish—and no one sees what is going on at sea, so any sort of control is difficult.

Fishy business

'Of all the fish that live in the sea, the herring is the one for me,' says an old folk song. The 'bonnie silver herring' has always been a kitchen favourite, whether smoked as kippers, pickled or grilled. It has been caught by Scottish fishermen in the North Sea and Atlantic Ocean for generations. During the 1970s, however, stocks in the North Sea became so depleted that herring fishing had to be banned entirely between 1977 and 1982. The cause for the fish's rapid decline was industrialised fishing: fine nets picked up juvenile and adult fish alike, giving stocks no chance to recover. During the period of the ban stocks rose, so that once again shoals of herring appeared in the North Sea. When fishing was restarted, legislation was introduced forbidding the landing of fish under 20 cm (eight inches) long in order to maintain stocks at sustainable levels.

The case of the herring shows that fish stocks can recover from overfishing, but that continued regulation and monitoring is necessary to prevent the landing of immature fish. But while attempts have been made to manage stocks of some fish, others have seen almost total collapse, as is the case with stocks of cod-icefish (a cod-like fish living in the South Seas) and the Peruvian anchovy.

In some cases overfishing can lead to imbalance in the ecosystem. Overfishing of mackerel and herring in the Atlantic, for example, led to a population 'flip'. Herring feed on sand eels and sand eels feed on herring larvae; therefore both species keep each other in check; mackerel, meanwhile, feed on the larvae of both herrings and sand eels. The overfishing of mackerel and herring led to a sudden and rapid increase in the number of sand eels. In the Antarctic worries have centred around the fishing of krill, which could put even more pressure on already hard pressed species such as whales—a 24-metre (80-foot) blue whale eats around 4 tonnes of krill per day. Almost every animal in the southern seas depends on krill in one way or another. Without it the Antarctic ecosystem would collapse. Luckily, krill is little exploited at present, as it is expensive to catch and difficult to convert into human food.

105

Blue-fin tuna at risk

Sky-high prices have always been bad news for wildlife. As the price of a particular animal product rises, the numbers of that species in the wild quickly dwindle. This has been true for white rhino, which is in extreme danger of extinction in the wild due to hunting for rhino horn, and for elephants, endangered in many areas due to ivory poaching. In the case of blue-fin tuna, prices of up to US $60,000 for a single fish could spell disaster. Japan consumes 40 per cent of the world's blue-fin catch, purchased mainly from Australia, the US, Taiwan, Spain and Canada. The two species of blue-fin tuna are the largest bony fish in the world, and are only found in the temperate waters of the Pacific and northern Atlantic oceans.

Save the whale

For the last 20 years people throughout the civilised world have been out-raged by the killing of whales. Despite a world moratorium on whaling, some hunting has continued in the name of scientific research. Since whale products are unnecessary, there can be little justification for the continued destruction of these beautiful mammals. The main countries which continue whaling are Norway and Japan. In the case of Norway, it is claimed that some of the small communities in the north of the country are dependent on whaling for their livelihoods. In Japan, whalemeat is regarded as a deli-cacy and fetches high prices, giving the whalers a strong financial incentive to carry on with their activities. Whales have a long breeding cycle, which means that it requires many years for stocks to be replenished.

Continued publicity over the killing of whales and dolphins has helped to keep large sea mammals in the news. During 1994 Greenpeace incurred large fines in Norway for trying to stop Norwegian whalers. But Greenpeace believes the fight is worthwhile in order to stop whaling for good.

WATER—TAKING ACTION

Everyone can help in the effort to clean up rivers, waterways and seas, both by being careful with their own use of water and by avoiding pollution.

Be careful how you use water

A number of obvious measures can help to reduce water consumption, including taking showers rather than baths and fitting water conserving toilets in your house. You should report any water leaks that you see to your local water authority—leaky pipes are one of the main ways in which water is wasted. You should avoid the use of garden sprinklers: in most temperate parts of the world, well-mulched soil—that is, soil with plenty of compost mixed in—will allow grass to survive in even the driest season. Equally, in vegetable gardens a richly composted soil will provide a better method of feeding and watering vegetables than the constant use of a hose pipe. Vegetables planted in this type of soil will only require watering during germination and establishment. If possible avoid the use of a hose pipe in your garden altogether, perhaps by using a large tub, tank or water butt to catch rainwater. Many plants appear to grow better when watered with rainwater than they do with tap water, which is chlorinated and often contains diluted mineral salts unsuitable for lime-hating plants such as heathers and rhododendrons.

There are many other ways of conserving water. One idea would be to carry out a water audit at home or at school or college to find out all the ways in which water is used, and to discover if consumption could be reduced.

Reducing pollution

Usually when people pollute water they are not really aware of what they are doing. Toxic substances poured down the drain can cause considerable damage to rivers and streams. This is particularly true of oil, which forms a thin film on the surface of water.

Old motor oil should ideally be taken to a recycling centre for reuse. It can also be used for cleaning your garden tools when you put them away for the winter. Some garages have facilities for oil recycling, but if such facilities are unavailable to you, then you should place your old engine oil in a sealed container and dispose of it safely. Avoid pouring all toxic chemicals, such as garden pesticides, down the drain.

You can lobby your local or national political representative by writing a letter, but there is no use in pretending that some of the acute problems faced by our rivers and seas can be tackled by personal action alone. Strict resolutions on emissions to streams and coastal waters, and rigorous enforcement of these regulations, are also necessary. Some countries have regulatory bodies such as the National Rivers Authority in the United Kingdom. If you are aware of any illegal discharges or serious instances of pollution, you should report them to these bodies, who then have a duty to act to stop the pollution occurring in the future. Perhaps one of the most irresponsible acts I have heard of was when a farmer dumped three large containers of DDT in a local river. This one act could cause untold damage for years to come. I am pleased to say that the farmer concerned was prosecuted, but it just goes to show how careless some people are.

107

ACTIVITIES

Investigate your local river or pond. As with air pollution, it is possible to monitor the pollution of your local stream or river using indicator species. Take care if you are undertaking this type of research, as some polluted water may pose a threat to human health. The species used for this type of survey will vary depending on whereabouts you live, and the velocity and depth of the water.

You will need the following equipment: fishing net, plastic bucket, collection trays, hand lens, sample tubes, stopwatch, metre rule, tape, pH testing kit.

1 Measure the depth of the stream using a metre rule, or a piece of string with a heavy weight attached.
2 Measure the speed or 'velocity' of the stream by timing how long it takes a bright floating object such as a coloured ball to float 10 metres.
3 Record the acidity or alkalinity of the water by performing a pH test. If you have not got the equipment to do one of these, a rough guide is that if your area is on chalk or limestone the water is likely to be alkaline; otherwise it is likely to be acidic.
4 Remove stones on the bottom to dislodge any animals, then hold the net under water, against the current, to collect any animals swimming in the flow. Empty your catch into the bucket. Have a look at the creatures that you have caught and try to identify them. Count the number of species present and record your results.

When carrying out this work try to make certain that you do not disturb any habitat that you are investigating. Replace live specimens in the water after you have finished.

Leaching experiments

You can construct a few interesting experiments to look at the movement of water through the soil and to help you understand how contaminants get into groundwater, and the problems of getting them out once they are there.

For this experiment you will need the following apparatus:

- 1 large, clear plastic tumbler, or lab beaker
- 1 50-cm (20-in) piece of plastic tubing
- waterproof sticky tape
- a disposable plastic syringe
- beach sand or washed river sand

108

✿ a coffee filter
✿ pebbles or clean gravel
✿ 1-cm (½ in) square piece of cloth
✿ food colouring or dyed oil
✿ a spray bottle or a watering can with rose attachment

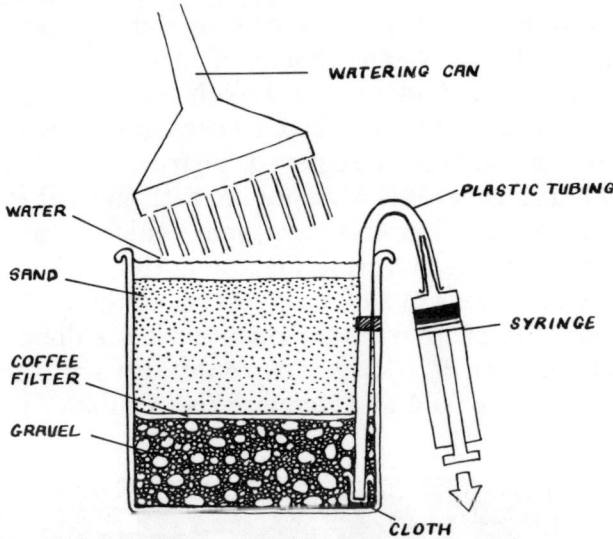

1 Make a filter by fastening a piece of cloth over one end of the plastic tubing. Secure the cloth well using tape.
2 Place the covered end of plastic tubing in the bottom of the lab beaker, and fasten it to the side.
3 Fill the first third of the lab beaker with the pebbles or gravel to represent bedrock.
4 Cover this layer with the coffee filter, to prevent the gravel getting mixed with the sand which will be placed on next.
5 Fill rest of cup to within 2.5 cm (1 in) of the top with washed river sand or sand from the beach to represent soil layers. Using clean sand avoids the problems of impurities from the sand entering the water.
6 With a spray bottle or watering can, simulate rain on the sand until water visibly filters down into the pebble or gravel layer.
7 Place the syringe in the open end of the plastic tube, and carefully draw the plunger out. The syringe represents a pump. As water fills it, your model starts working.

The next stage is to contaminate the water to find out what happens. To represent contaminants you can use either food colouring or a solvent mixed with dye. If you are using solvent, make certain you dispose of the experiment properly once you have finished—don't throw your solvent down the sink. Place the colouring agent on top of the sand to represent contaminants. Water the sand with your spray or watering can as described earlier, pump out the coloured water and repeat the raining effect.

You can repeat this experiment with a number of different substances and compare the results. You will notice that some materials leach more easily than others. Although experiments of this type are not as accurate as experiments carried out under natural conditions, they nevertheless give a good idea of how groundwater can become contaminated and how difficult it is for those contaminants to be removed. Bear in mind that groundwater supplies are often a considerable distance beneath the soil surface and that contaminants take a long time to reach them, which means that they are held in the soil to continue polluting for a long time after they have been deposited. If you have access to advanced testing equipment, you could compare the leaching rate of ammonium nitrate with sulphate of potash or other ingredients used in fertiliser. You could also try leaching different soil samples taken in the field and compare the results.

7   Energy Use and Transport

If you are interested in energy issues, you are onto a winner. Saving energy benefits almost everybody. Businesses can cut costs through energy efficiency measures, as can you, your family, your school and college, and nearly every public utility. On a national basis, energy imports are expensive, financially as well as environmentally. Gobbling up our precious reserves of fossil fuels is in no one's best long-term interests. Using energy more efficiently is probably one of the biggest challenges our society faces today. Energy use is at the heart of a whole range of environmental issues: it is linked to global warming, acid rain, air pollution and water pollution.

International efforts to save energy and to develop technologies to capture renewable resources such as wind and wave power have helped to reduce our reliance on fossil fuels—but not much. We still have an enormous way to go to check the twentieth-century trend which has seen the burning of ever-increasing quantities of fossil fuels, let alone to reverse it. Current international efforts have tended to focus on stabilising levels of greenhouse-gas emissions rather than reducing them. For example, in April 1993 US president Bill Clinton announced a plan to reduce emissions to their 1990 level by the year 2000. The UK has set the same target. Given the steady increase in fossil-fuel use throughout the century, this is a move in the right direction, but many environmentalists say that it barely scratches the surface. In contrast to the US and the UK, Denmark is aiming to reduce CO_2 emissions by 20 per cent by the year 2000 (see Chapter 5).

Ultimately, successful initiatives must be developed locally as well as nationally and internationally, so there is plenty of scope for you to get involved. Due to the increasing awareness of the issues there has never been a better time to develop new and better methods of using and producing energy. Don't be put off from learning more about energy issues because of some of the heavy physics involved in the technical issues related to energy. Luckily for most of us, understanding how to save energy is a lot easier than understanding physics. Efforts really centre around using available resources to the maximum effect and reducing waste.

So what are the issues surrounding our use of energy, and how can we set about reducing our impact on the environment? I have two points to make before I attempt to answer these questions. Firstly, very few people truly realise how dependent they are on energy use. Almost every aspect of our daily lives involves using energy in one form or another—getting around, moving any resource from A to B, manufacturing processes, heating and running domestic appliances all rely on using imported energy in one form or another, which is why energy use is linked to so many other issues. Secondly, all energy production has some impact on the environment. Even the 'green methods' of producing energy have some negative impact. This has become a particularly controversial issue, with disputes arising over the siting of hydroelectric plants, tidal barrages and wind farms. The challenge we face is to reduce the environmental impact of energy production to a minimum. The obvious first step to doing this is to promote the efficient use of energy on a global basis, which is the single measure most likely to bring speedy environmental benefits. At the end of the day, reducing our energy consumption comes down to organising our economy in such a way that resources are used effectively. You don't need to be an environmentalist to see that this makes sense.

Powerhouse in the sky

The sun is the source of nearly all of our energy. Every half-hour, the earth receives more energy from the sun than is released by all the fossil fuels burnt in the world for a whole year. The different heating of different parts of Earth influences the movement of air and ocean currents. The sun's energy warms the atmosphere and provides 'fuel' for plants through the process of photosynthesis. Nearly all other forms of life, with a few rare exceptions, ultimately rely on the food energy provided by plants, algae and other photosynthesising organisms. So the sun lies at the heart of all earth's life.

Over millions of years some of the energy captured by plants has been stored in the form of fossil fuels, which were formed from the remains of dead plants and animals. Such fuels are highly useful because of the concentrated form in which the energy is held, and the speed with which it can be converted into other forms of energy. Our modern industrial world is, therefore, heavily dependent on the supply of fossil fuels. In countries such as the US and Britain, around 90 per cent of all primary energy is supplied by burning fossil fuels. Other sources of energy include wind, hydroelectricity, nuclear power and the power supplied by waves, tides and geothermal energy.

There is a huge global energy disparity between rich and poor. The big gas-guzzling nations of the world are the rich industrial nations of the northern hemisphere. The United States produces on average around 5 tonnes of carbon dioxide per person per year, the United Kingdom around 3 tonnes and West Germany around 3.5 tonnes. By contrast, the average citizen of countries such as India and China produces less than 0.5 tonnes of CO_2 per year. So, while it is right that developing nations should be encouraged to develop fuel-efficient economies, our first priority should be to get the richer countries of the world to use their energy resources to better effect.

Useful energy

A revealing way of thinking about the way we use energy is to concentrate on what we are using it for. The more of the primary energy source transformed into usable energy for heating, cooking, transport, and so on, the more efficient our use of energy will be, whether it comes from coal, oil or wind power.

It seems amazing that the average coal-fired power station converts only around 35 per cent of its energy into electricity—even more of which is wasted once it reaches the home. Many power stations burning fossil fuels produce huge amounts of hot water which are just left to cool. The most common method of generating electricity is through steam turbines: fuel is burned to heat water, and the resulting steam is forced through a barrel to turn the blades of the turbine. The problem with this system is that the steam requires cooling after use, turning it back once again into water. This cooling process requires large quantities of water which is then allowed to cool in towers. With a little ingenuity it is possible to use this hot water usefully, for heating municipal buildings, for example, in what are often known as district heating schemes, thus saving most of the energy. This is a technique called combined heat and power or CHP. Helsinki in Finland uses combined heat and power to heat 80 per cent of the city's homes. If this was repeated throughout the world, the energy saving would be enormous.

But is it practical to reduce our energy use? Well, it would be useless to pretend that we could solve our problems overnight. Our current infrastructure is geared to high-energy consumption, so even if we give it our best effort we are likely to be dependent on fossil fuels for some time to come.

113

Change will be a long and slow process, but countries can save energy if they try. The United States, for example, has a reputation as one of the most energy-intensive economies on earth. However, in response to the oil shortage of 1973, the US took measures greatly to improve its energy efficiency. The result was that the country was able to cut its oil use by 13 million barrels a day. Between 1973 and 1986, the American economy grew 35 per cent while energy use remained at the same level. Despite such improvements, however, the US still uses twice as much energy as Japan per unit of economic output: if it reached Japanese levels of efficiency, the country would save a further $220 billion annually. These savings would be distributed among many households and companies, helping to make industrial processes more cost-effective and reducing reliance on expensive energy imports, to the potential benefit of the whole economy.

ENERGY EFFICIENCY—THE SAVINGS

In the United Kingdom, government figures show that energy efficiency measures could reduce energy use by 60 per cent. Potential savings could be made in two areas, the most significant of which is by improving the insulation of buildings using existing technology. The energy used to heat an average family home in a temperate climate could be reduced by up to 70 per cent through careful insulation. The second area for potential reductions is through the use of energy-efficient goods. A compact fluorescent light bulb, for example, gives the same amount of light as a normal tungsten bulb, using one fifth of the energy. Some fridges use a third of the energy used by others of the same size, largely through better insulation. Carelessness is another area in which savings could be made. If all the TV sets left on standby—when they still use electricity—were switched off, enough energy would be saved in a country such as the UK or a state such as California to close down a power station. Some of the activities at the end of this chapter concentrate on promoting energy efficiency. Why not conduct the energy survey and work out how much your family could save?

Energy-efficient computers

Energy-efficient computers have received a lot of publicity, but how much difference do they really make? More energy-efficient machines mean fewer greenhouse gases released into the atmosphere, which is comforting for concerned computer users. According to IBM, the world's largest computer manufacturer, a business using 100 PS/2 E machines nine hours a day, five days a week, could save about US $2,000 a year. In a country such as

Switzerland, where electricity rates are higher, savings would rise. The computer's cover is made of recycled plastic, which makes sense when you remember that the average computer is upgraded every two to five years and that plastic is non-biodegradable.

ELECTRICITY GENERATION

Fossil fuels

Around a third of all fossil fuels burnt in the developed world are used to generate electricity. Coal-burning power stations are particularly polluting, producing both sulphur dioxide and nitrogen oxides, gases which are a major cause of acid rain. But all fossil-fuel-burning power stations produce CO_2, the main greenhouse gas. Bearing in mind the low efficiency of these stations, the environmental costs look a high price to pay.

Nuclear power

In the 1960s and '70s nuclear power was sold as the energy source of the future. It seemed to have a lot to commend it—it was promoted as being clean, cheap and safe, and a genuine long-term alternative to fossil fuels. So what went wrong? One problem was that few people considered the potential environmental effects of a nuclear disaster. Nor did it occur to many people that some countries might develop nuclear power as a first step to developing nuclear weapons. The acute concern that has since centred around the nuclear programmes of Iraq and North Korea shows that this was a big mistake. And what of radioactive waste? People were less conscious of the waste-disposal issue in the 1960s, so it was largely glossed over. Nobody seemed to give much thought to how you disposed of substances that remain radioactive for 10,000 years. As a result, some countries developed adventurous nuclear power programmes: France, for example, produces 80 per cent of its electricity from nuclear power.

Two things that helped change the public's attitude to nuclear power were the disaster at Chernobyl nuclear power station in the then Soviet Union, and the realisation that atomic energy was actually not cheap at all. It costs around twice as much to generate electricity from nuclear power as it does from coal-fired power stations, even without considering the enormous sums required for decommissioning nuclear stations when they become obsolete. It now seems increasingly unlikely that many new nuclear power stations will spring up to replace the old ones as they are abandoned. Certainly, very few countries will be looking to increase their nuclear capacity.

115

In short, nuclear power is too dangerous, and too expensive. Yet, despite this, the nuclear lobby remains strong, and many existing programmes receive enormous subsidies. If the huge amounts of funding attracted by the nuclear industry had been spent on researching and developing renewable resources, who knows what advances could have been made?

What is perhaps most alarming is that developing nations such as India have been tempted to invest in nuclear electricity. When one considers the outrageously high costs and the small benefit to often rural populations, these schemes seem the opposite of what is needed in such a situation.

I do not intend to go into all the arguments for and against nuclear power—that would require a whole book. If you are interested in nuclear issues it is worth reading widely from both sides of the debate, and discussing the issues with a group of friends or fellow students.

The day the nuclear bubble burst

In April 1986 a massive explosion at the Chernobyl nuclear power plant in the Ukraine sent a radioactive cloud into the air which drifted across a large part of Western and Eastern Europe, affecting regions as far apart as the eastern Mediterranean and Arctic Scandinavia. Reindeer in Lapland and sheep in Wales were too radioactive to eat for several years after the accident. Much of the land in the immediate vicinity of the plant will be seriously contaminated for many years to come, and unfit for human habitation. No one knows how many fatalities will eventually result because of the Chernobyl disaster, but it has been estimated that up to 100,000 people could die prematurely in the former Soviet Union alone over the next 40 years.

The Apache and the nuclear dump

A proposed new nuclear dump on the Mescalero Apache reservation in southern New Mexico could help the American nuclear industry survive. A severe problem has arisen in the US over the storage of nuclear waste. By 1998, a quarter of the country's nuclear plants will have run out of storage space for their radioactive waste, possibly leading to the premature closure of plants, because many communities are unwilling to have nuclear dumps in their area and many existing dumps plan to reduce their intake of waste. Some 32 nuclear plants from 27 states are looking to the Mescalero Apache tribe for rescue.

Since billions of dollars have been invested in the American nuclear industry, a strong financial incentive exists to construct the plant. A larger plant in the Yucca mountains in Nevada will not come on stream until the year 2010, so the Mescalero site is seen as an important interim measure. The Mescalero themselves hope to create job opportunities in an area where chronic unemployment is a problem. Since the tribe has a right to decide on the use to which reservation land is put, there is little that state politicians can do to stop the dump going ahead. Schemes such as this seem to offer an escape from disadvantage to people such as the Native Americans, but because, under US law, Native American tribes are considered sovereign nations, such plans also represent a type of pollution export.

ALTERNATIVE SOURCES OF ENERGY

Wind, waves, the sun, hydroelectric and geothermal heat: by now probably everyone knows something about these renewable sources of energy. But do they really offer an alternative? In theory we would only need to capture 0.05 per cent of the world's wind energy in order to supply all the energy the human race currently uses. In practice, developing renewable energy resources is likely to take some time and will have to go hand in hand with energy conservation measures if we are to make a significant move away from our reliance on fossil fuels. Nevertheless, in the last ten years much has been done to promote and develop renewable sources of energy, often by small groups of people working with little or no government funding. The challenge now is to take some of these initiatives forward and make a positive step in the direction of protecting our environment.

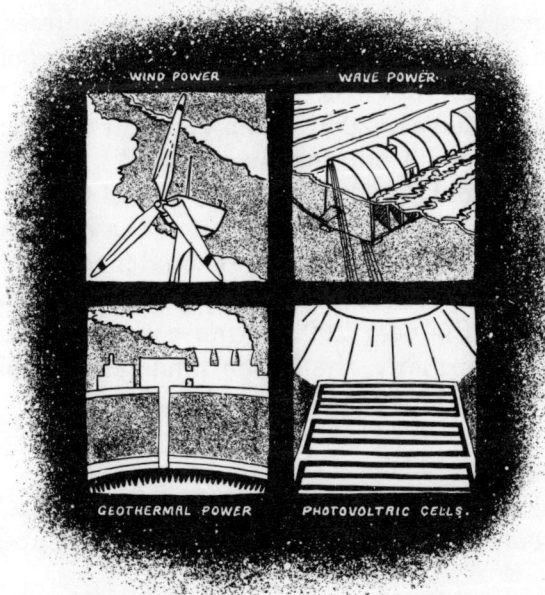

So what are the alternatives and how viable are they? Let's look at some of alternative sources of power and their effectiveness.

Wind power

People have used wind energy in one form or another for thousands of years. It may appear that we have moved on a long way since the days of windmills and three-masted ships, and yet it is surprising that our society has done so little to exploit such an obvious and readily available resource. It was not until 1941 that wind energy was fed into the electricity grid, when a 33-metre wind generator was built on a small hill in Vermont, USA. This strange, 250-tonne contraption, known locally as Grandpa's Knob, produced enough electricity to supply 1,200 homes for four years, before being damaged in a storm.

Technology has moved on since 1941, and today's leaner wind generators are beginning once again to play a role in the business of electricity generation. Although wind generators, on their own, cannot replace fossil-burning power stations, in many parts of the world they are beginning to play an important role in the development of an alternative energy strategy. In the UK, a country of 60 million people, it is estimated that 20 to 35 per cent of electricity supplies could be generated by wind power.

California and Denmark

The two parts of the world where wind power has been most exploited are the USA and Denmark. In California, good wind resources and government subsidies have led to the state producing more than 1 per cent of its electricity using wind power, and it is hoped that this capacity will increase to around 4 per cent by the year 2000. Wind generators in the USA currently have a capacity of around 1,600 megawatts (MW). It is hoped to increase this to between 4,000 and 8,000 MW by the end of the century. This, however, would still only meet a small fraction of the country's energy needs. Denmark, home to the world's first offshore wind farm at Vindeby, currently produces around 455 MW of electricity using wind generators, and aims to produce 1,000 MW by the year 2000. Other countries currently exploiting wind energy include Germany, the Netherlands and China.

Wave power

The generation of electrical power using the waves has great potential. Capturing wave energy is still a poorly researched area, and although schemes have been investigated in Norway and elsewhere, a lot of research is still needed before the large-scale generation of electricity from waves becomes practical. That said, many coastal areas could benefit from the use of wave power.

Hydroelectricity

Hydroelectricity—using running water to create power—is one of the cheapest methods of generating electricity, costing around one and a half cents or one penny per unit. Hydroelectric power stations currently supply a quarter of the world's electricity—more than nuclear power. In some countries, hydroelectric power is the main source of electricity, as, for example, in Norway. For countries with high, barren mountains with fast-running rivers and lakes, hydroelectricity makes sense. But sometimes the environmental costs of building a hydroelectric station exceed the benefits, as in some cases in the Amazonian area of Brazil. The Amazon lies in a plain, so huge areas of land have to be flooded in order to build up the necessary water pressure to generate electricity. Flooding sensitive areas not only destroys huge tracts of rainforest, but also destroys the homes of many native peoples.

Biomass

Wood, straw and domestic waste can all be burned to produce heat and electricity, as can gas from sewage works and landfill sites. In the case of domestic waste, recycling and reuse are better than either incineration or landfilling, but where landfill sites already exist extracting methane gas makes good sense.

Biofuel can be made from sugar-producing plants. In Brazil, alcohol produced in this way is used to help fuel the nation's cars. Because it gives off recently synthesised carbon dioxide, biofuel is a renewable source of energy. When the crop is grown again the following year, it absorbs an equivalent amount of CO_2. Biofuel may sound great, apparently promising a way of continuing with our extravagant use of energy. Unfortunately, to produce sufficient quantities of biofuel to meet the world's current energy needs would require enormous areas of our most fertile land to be planted with fuel-growing crops. All the same, biofuel will become more important in the future.

Tidal power

In tidal estuaries, barrages can be used to hold water during times of low tide, when the trapped water escapes through turbines, producing electricity. Unfortunately many estuaries are also important for wildlife, so the siting of barrages needs very careful consideration.

Geothermal heat

Geothermal energy uses heat from the earth's core to produce electricity, and is particularly useful in areas of the world where volcanic activity is above average. If water is pumped deep below the ground in these places, it becomes hot and produces steam, which can then be used to drive turbines. Worldwide, more than 250 geothermal plants are in operation, with a total planned capacity of 13,000 megawatts. Natural steam resources provide California with almost 7 per cent of its electricity. The California Energy Company's Coso Geothermal Project currently produces 240 megawatts— enough electricity to meet the needs of 240,000 southern California households.

Solar power

Although the sun produces an enormous amount of energy, it is only possible to capture the tiniest proportion for direct use. Nevertheless, solar power may provide a workable alternative to burning fossil fuels in sunny areas of the world, where solar technology has been developed in parts of Australia, the US, Israel and Japan.

Solar energy can be used for heating or to convert sunlight directly into electricity by using a technology called photovoltaics, which are commonly used to produce electricity in remote areas lacking power lines and for powering space satellites. Another form of solar energy, called solar thermal, produces heat and electricity by concentrating sunlight on a receiver containing fluid. The heated fluid runs through pipes submerged in water, creating steam to power an electric turbine. Solar panels can be used on houses to provide hot water, usually again using solar thermal technology, which is a viable method of saving energy even in cooler climates. Improvements in solar technology over the past 15 years have greatly reduced its cost, and solar energy may soon be competitive with conventional sources, especially if environmental costs are included.

Passive solar heating

Huge amounts of energy can be saved simply by designing houses to catch more of the sun's energy. Large south-facing windows using the best types of double glazing allow heat from the sun to enter the house, while still providing adequate insulation. Although the knowledge and technology to build these houses has existed for some time, very few new homes maximise the potential of passive solar heating.

The cost of renewable resources

Several factors make it difficult to estimate the cost of producing electricity from renewable resources. First, the main cost of renewable energy resources is investment in capital equipment. Once the equipment is in place, the main costs are maintenance, the fuel itself being free. By contrast, the main cost of producing electricity using fossil fuels is the cost of the fuel itself. A second difficulty in comparing the cost of producing electricity generated using fossil fuels with renewable energy is the environmental cost. Burning fossil fuels has a far higher environmental cost than producing energy from most renewable resources. If power companies had to pay this environmental cost there is no doubt that many would quickly invest in renewable research and development.

Hydroelectricity provides the cheapest way of producing electricity at around one and a half cents (one penny) per kilowatt-hour, or unit. Fossil fuels produce electricity at around five cents (three and a half pence) per kilowatt-hour and wind power may cost around nine cents (six pence) per kilowatt-hour. Without taking into account environmental cost, wind power looks more expensive than coal and natural gas, but it is still far cheaper than nuclear power, which costs around 15 cents (ten pence) per kilowatt-hour, and perhaps far more if decommissioning nuclear stations is taken into account.

TRANSPORT

One of the most difficult environmental questions we face today is how to reduce our reliance on the motor car. People love cars. Children play with toy cars, adults see cars as extensions of their families and identities. Cars are big business: every town and every country wants to produce them. Yet the seemingly endless increase in the number of cars on the road causes severe air-pollution problems, depletes many urban environments, causes loss of life and injury through road traffic accidents, adds to global warming

121

and poses an unprecedented threat to many ecosystems through continued road building. But many people would view any move to reduce the number of cars on the road as a restriction in personal freedom. Our societies have become so reliant on the car that many people would have severe difficulty coping without them. Children often have to be transported by car over even short distances, due to the risk of walking along or across busy main roads.

Environmentalists still have a long way to go to win the arguments for restricting the number of cars on the road. Many politicians are afraid to be associated with anything which smacks of restricting personal liberty, or which is likely to be unpopular with the public at large. Quite a few still see road building as environmental improvement rather than environmental degradation. However, in some parts of the world, the problems posed by traffic have become so bad that authorities have been forced to act. For example, in Singapore tolls are imposed on all cars in the city centre carrying less than four people. In Odense in Denmark traffic-calming measures have reduced the number of hospital admissions.

Measures such as these are a start, but we still have a long way to go to free our society from addiction to the motor car. Compulsory use of catalytic converters to reduce the toxic effects of exhaust fumes will help to alleviate some of the air-pollution problems caused by motor vehicles, but the ever-increasing numbers of cars and lorries means that catalytic converters are only likely to offer temporary respite. They do nothing to tackle the underlying problem. To do that we need to reduce the total number of vehicles on the road.

Case study: Transport in India

In India as elsewhere air pollution is a serious problem in many cities. Surprisingly the culprit is not the motor car, but the enormous numbers of mopeds, scooters and motorbikes that whizz along the country's roads. In all, India has more than 15 million of these vehicles, making up almost 80 per cent of the country's vehicle production. They consume around two-thirds of the fuel used for transportation. Currently many of these motor cycles have inefficient two-stroke engines making them heavy on petrol and emitting a lot of exhaust fumes.

A project started by WWF-India in 1992 promotes the use of cleaner technology in the Indian motorcycle industry. WWF hopes to reduce fuel consumption and air pollution by working together with companies such as TVS-Sazuki, who have developed a fuel-injected two-stroke engine that offers improvements in fuel efficiency and reduced hydrocarbon emissions. This type of technological transfer programme is particularly beneficial to

122

developing nations and helps towards reducing emissions of greenhouse gases.

Take action

Why not get some sort of discussion going at a local level, even if only among your friends and family? This will help, because unhooking ourselves from reliance on the automobile is still at the hearts-and-minds phase. Lobby on individual road-building schemes or on issues of air pollution by writing letters to national and local politicians. Contact your local authority and find out what is being done locally to introduce traffic-calming measures.

Try to persuade the people in your home and school to:

- Buy the most efficient light bulbs (small fluorescent or halogen bulbs).
- Buy the most energy-efficient models of appliances.
- Avoid electricity if installing new heating.
- Check the loft has at least 15 cm (6 ins) of insulation and that hot-water tanks and pipes are lagged.
- Fit draught-proofing around door frames and badly fitting windows. Consider secondary glazing. As much as one-quarter of a house's heat is lost through draughts.
- Turn down central heating thermostats, if your home or school has them—a one degree centigrade drop could lower annual fuel use by as much as 10 per cent.
- Think about fitting a shower – they use half as much heated water as a bath.
- Try to reduce the number of car miles you travel by either using public transport or alternative means such as a bicycle.
- When using a kettle, only boil the amount of water you actually need and save energy.
- Recycle paper. Production of recycled paper uses 60 per cent less energy than production of virgin paper.

ACTIVITIES

Finding hot and cold spots

Conduct a temperature survey of your school to discover the hot and cold spots; this is also useful for air-conditioned buildings where you insulate against heat entering the building rather than escaping. By finding the hot and cold spots you should be able to find out where energy problems are occurring. Place a series of thermometers around the building to be surveyed. Check the temperatures three times a day: first thing in the morning, at around 1 p.m. and at the end of the day. Take readings over a period of at least a week. Plot your results for each area on a spreadsheet and calculate the average temperature for each area.

When surveying energy use it is useful to convert your energy into kilowatt-hours. This allows you to compare the proportion of energy used for one particular application with that used for another, for example comparing space heating as against lighting and the use of electrical appliances. It may also help you find out where the biggest potential savings could be made. If you care to do a few more calculations you could work out the energy efficiency factor for your home, school or college, using a teaching pack from the Centre for Sustainable Energy (address at the back of this book).

Here are the calculations for converting units for a range of fuels into kilowatt-hours:

Natural gas:	therms × 29.31 = kWh
	Cu feet × 0.303 = kWh
Gas oil:	litres × 10.6 = kWh
Light fuel oil:	litres × 11.2 = kWh
Medium fuel oil:	litres × 11.3 = kWh
Heavy fuel oil:	litres × 1.4 = kWh
Coal:	tonnes × 7600 = kWh
Anthracite:	tonnes × 9200 = kWh
Liquid petroleum gas:	litres × 7 = kWh

A simple energy audit

It is surprising how much energy efficiency varies between different households. Differences in home insulation are one reason, but some people are just more careful with energy than others. One good way to find out how you use energy and what you can do to cut your consumption is to carry out a simple energy audit.

Make a list of all the uses of energy in your home, not forgetting to include things such as the direct burning of fuel for heating. You might include household appliances such as cookers, washing machines and vacuum cleaners, lights, water heating and so on. For each item, decide whether energy consumption could be reduced.

Here are some questions that might help you to find some of the energy-wasting areas of your home or school.

HOME

Is the roof insulated?

Are the wall cavities insulated?

Are the rooms heated by gas?

Are the rooms heated by electric fires?

Are there electric night storage heaters?

Are the windows double-glazed?

Is the hot-water system insulated?

Is the front door draughty?

Do you have ordinary tungsten bulbs?

Have you fitted compact fluorescent bulbs?

If you live in a warm part of the world, do you keep air conditioning to a minimum?

SCHOOL/COLLEGE

Are lights left on in empty classrooms?

Are more lights used than are needed?

Are outside doors kept closed during winter?

Are any hot taps dripping?

Are there any rooms which are too cold?

Are windows left open in winter?

Do radiators have individual thermostats?

Are there notices in the school asking that lights be turned off?

Are drinks cans thrown away or recycled?

If you wanted to take this survey work even further you might look at factors such as the architecture of your home. Energy-efficient homes often have large, south-facing windows, designed to capture the sun's energy. In some hot parts of the world, raising a house on a series of short stilts is a method used for keeping it cool.

Once you have looked at the energy efficiency of your home, why not work out how much CO_2 you or your family are producing? You can work this out approximately using the following table.

1 kWh electricity = 1 kg (2.2 lb) CO_2
1 therm gas   = 5.3 kg (11.6 lb) CO_2
1 kg (2.2 lb) coal = 2.95 kg (6.49 lb) CO_2

1 kg (2.2 lb) CO_2 has a volume of 500 litres.

Monitor your energy consumption over a week and then multiply the result by 52. This will give you some idea of how much CO_2 you produce annually.

Implement some ideas for conserving energy and then repeat your estimate of CO_2 produced per year. If you have thought out a good programme, you should be producing noticeably less.

This same exercise can be carried out at school or college as well as at home.

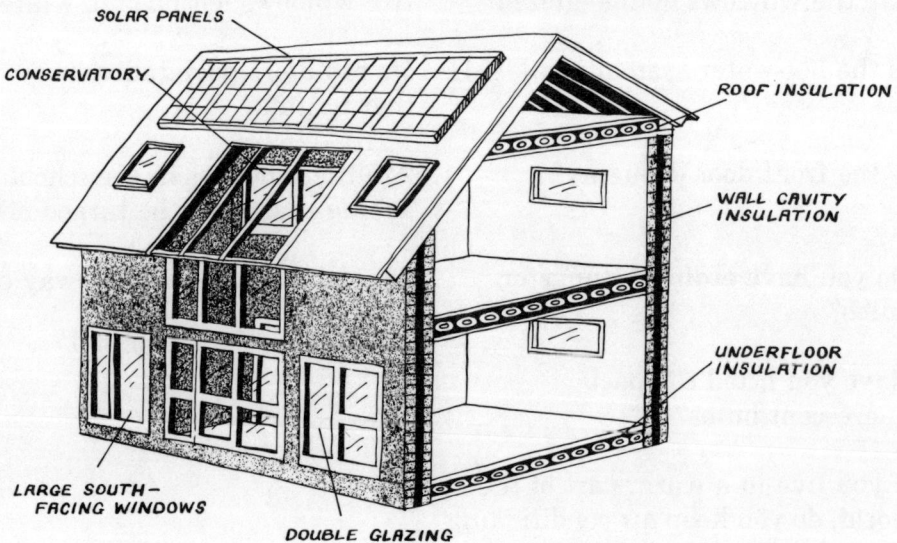

126

Build a solar house

If you are interested in design or architecture, you could try designing your own solar house. Build a model and see how it compares with a model of a house using a standard design by measuring the internal temperature (remember to standardise the conditions and position of the thermometer). You can use a pair of standard lamps to represent the sun—these will need to be placed an equal distance from the models and the external temperature checked to ensure that the conditions are equal.

8 At the Shops

Protecting the environment goes beyond simply what we buy at the shops to include our patterns of consumption and what we do with things after we have bought them. All the same, many consumers find it difficult to sort out all the claims of manufacturers, which often have more to do with selling products than with protecting the environment. On the other hand, some manufacturers have made genuine efforts to change. So how can you tell which is which?

The first thing to understand is that all manufacturing activity has some impact on the environment. It is difficult to see how consumption on today's scale can be sustainable without massive efforts being made to recycle and reuse the waste we produce, and also to reduce energy consumption. The challenge for an environmentally aware manufacturer is to reduce the environmental impact as much as possible. Some companies have made efforts to do this, but it is often difficult for them because of worries about losing their competitive edge, which might happen if their competitors do not do the same. Not all manufacturers are starting from a level playing field. That is why national and international legislation is so important.

From the consumer's point of view, making wise choices for the environment can only really come from understanding the issues. The first message that any environmentally aware consumer must understand is consume less: for the wise consumer, quality is better than quantity. Goods built to last are not only sensible from an economic point of view, but are also sensible from an environmental point of view. For example, purchasing a low-energy compact fluorescent light bulb does not only reduce your energy

128

consumption: such bulbs also have a far greater life expectancy than conventional bulbs, and therefore save resources.

Take action

The other chapters of this book should give you some clues as to how you can judge the claims of manufacturers (see for example the four Rs of recycling in Chapter 2). But here are a few more useful tips.

- Avoid buying wood from tropical rainforests.
- Purchase recycled paper.
- Avoid overwrapped goods.
- Buy milk in returnable bottles if possible.
- Purchase energy-efficient electrical goods and encourage others to do the same. Remember that a greater contribution to the environment can be made through energy efficiency than through almost any other means.
- Avoid using aerosols if possible. All aerosols are wasteful of resources, even though most don't now contain CFCs. If possible buy pump-action refillable sprays.
- Ask your parents to avoid purchasing artificial garden chemicals.
- Encourage your parents to buy organically grown food where it is available.
- Don't believe all the claims that manufacturers make: work out if they are true for yourself.

BEAUTY WITH KINDNESS

Over the years there has been increasing concern about the use of animals in the safety testing of a wide range of products. This concern has been especially acute in the case of cosmetics, since many people believe that it is unnecessary and label it as 'cruelty for vanity'. Today there are many cosmetics on the market made from natural products tried and tested over many years, and although it would be unsafe to assume that these products have never been tested on animals, it is fair to say with quite a number of products that they are no longer tested on animals. Many companies operate a cruelty-free labelling scheme: this does not mean, however, that they do not use animals for testing other products. If you feel strongly about this issue, the best way of finding out more about which products to purchase is to contact one of the animal-rights organisations at the end of this book. One of the best-known suppliers of cruelty-free products is the Body Shop, which has branches in more than 30 different countries. The Body Shop has a policy of selling no product tested on animals within the last five years, and also uses minimum packaging and encourages recycling.

ANIMAL TESTING

Three common animal tests used by manufacturers to assess the safety of products are set out below:

Toxicity tests

(Including the LD50 procedure.) A group of animals—usually small mammals such as mice or rats—are force-fed with a product until 50 per cent die. This test is used with a wide range of household and garden products.

Tests for eye irritation

The Draize test uses conscious rabbits for testing levels of eye irritation. Rabbits are unable to flush irritating substances away from their eyes because of the way that their tear ducts are structured. These tests are often repeated over several days to see if the eyes are damaged. This test is one that has particularly outraged animal-rights activists.

Tests for skin irritation

Animals such as rabbits and pigs have areas of skin shaved and substances held against the skin with tape to see if the skin shows signs of irritation.

Animal products and cosmetics

Many cosmetics are made from animal products, and are therefore unsuitable for use by anyone who is a vegetarian. These products include tallow which is made from animal fat and used in soaps and lipsticks, and products such as gelatine, made from the boiled-down bones, gristle and skin of animals. In some cases, products are derived from rare species, including squalene, an oil from basking sharks which is used in a wide range of products such as face creams.

VEGETARIANISM

I am not going to go into all the arguments for and against vegetarianism here, but many people see it as an important part of a greener life style.

Certainly, if more people were vegetarian a greater proportion of primary food products would enter the human food chain, relieving pressure on land and reducing the need for intensive agricultural production. A number of good resources are available promoting a vegetarian life style (see the back of the book for addresses).

THE COST OF CONSCIOUSNESS

One of the criticisms often levelled at environmental legislation is that it can make companies less competitive and therefore less profitable. However, the annual report of Japan's Environmental Agency published in May 1994 predicts that investment in environmental projects will benefit the economy and create jobs. The report predicts that eco-business such as the development of technologies to reduce pollution and improvements to infrastructure such as sewage treatment will grow by 8 per cent by the year 2000.

TOXIC SUBSTANCES IN YOUR HOME

A surprising number of substances found in the average household contain highly toxic ingredients.

Cadmium: Cadmium is a carcinogen, meaning it can produce cancer. It is also associated with respiratory irritation, kidney damage and, in animals, damage to the liver and central nervous system. Any product containing cadmium, such as rechargeable batteries, should be treated with care and disposed of carefully.

131

Cresol: Cresol is an aromatic product derived from phenol used in many products, including antiseptics and disinfectants. It is also found in coal tar and creosote. Cresol is very corrosive to all tissues; prolonged exposure to or repeated absorption of even low concentrations may cause chronic systemic poisoning.

Lye: Lye—sodium hydroxide or potassium hydroxide (caustic soda)—is a white, highly alkaline substance. In its concentrated form it is corrosive to all bodily tissues, causing burns and frequently deep ulceration. Eye contact can cause severe damage to delicate tissue. Sodium hydroxide is used in the manufacture of soap, aluminium, rayon and paper.

Paraquat: An extremely poisonous weedkiller, used as a defoliant for its ability to destroy chlorophyll. Fatal if ingested in sufficient quantities. Paraquat is restricted in many countries.

Pine oil: Pine oil is used in a wide range of disinfectants and other household products. It is irritating to eyes and mucous membranes. In some people it can produce an allergic reaction. If ingested it can have a range of harmful effects, including weakness, depression and kidney irritation.

2, 4-D: This is a chemical found in selective weedkillers. This chemical is persistent and has long been suspected of having harmful side effects. In animals it causes liver and kidney damage.

This list only contains a few common chemicals found in household products. If you suspect a product of being corrosive or potentially harmful, store and handle it carefully. Always wear protective clothing such as gloves and eye protection when handling corrosive substances. Even better, look for a less harmful alternative. *The Green Consumer Guide* by John Elkington and Julia Hailes contains useful information on common products and their alternatives.

Computing and the environment

A computer is a handy tool for working on environmental projects. Many modern word processors can plot graphs, draw pictures, including maps, and perform many other useful functions. However, whichever way you look at it, computers use energy and resources. Reducing the amount of energy used by computers is both possible and desirable. Some computers have special energy-saving devices to make them more energy efficient, so if you are buying a new computer, go for one with low energy consumption. If you already have a computer and you are looking to upgrade it, then DIY options

132

save resources. Low energy motherboards are available on the market, and cost little more than those using far more energy. But the best advice is to keep your old computer unless you really need to upgrade it. If you must change, you may think of giving your old computer to a school or charity able to make good use of it.

Some obvious measures can help reduce energy. Here are a few ideas:

- Print on both sides of your paper. If your printer is unable to do this, then reuse old paper for draft copies, remembering to take out any staples first.
- Use recycled paper for your work.
- Switch off your computer when not in use. Modern computers will not be damaged by switching them on and off. If you can't switch your computer off, turn off the monitor.
- There is no evidence to show that radiation from computer monitors is bad for your health, but you should certainly give your eyes a change every couple of hours by having a ten-minute break from computer work. Low-radiation monitors are desirable as a precaution. Use a wrist-rest for typing to help avoid repetitive strain injury (RSI).
- Noise from computers is rarely seen as a problem, but the constant whirr of computer fans and hard disks can become annoying and lower your productivity. Some of this noise can be reduced by putting the main body of your computer under a surface. If you are buying a new computer, it is worth bearing in mind that some are far quieter than others.
- Join one of the many good environmental computer networks such as GreenNet in the United Kingdom. These provide access to global gold mines of information, and can save hours of time for anyone researching a particular topic. One tip, though: get some training. Computer networks are rarely user-friendly, unless you know exactly what you are doing. Computer networks are also handy if you want to zap a few aliens without spending megabucks on over-packaged software, and there are some very good environmental packages around too. Shareware games are readily available over the Net, many of which are very sophisticated and often developed by new and emerging businesses. The shareware system is a sort of 'on approval' method of acquiring software—if you like what you see, you can register it and receive the full package, which saves spending your hard-earned money on stuff you don't really need.

ACTIVITIES

Check up on what you are buying before you make a purchase. Ask yourself a few critical questions before you act. The first should always be: 'Do I really need it?'

Find out more about toxic substances in the home

Many ingredients used in common household products are not listed on the packaging. Why not conduct a survey of your house, listing the items used in your kitchen, garage, garden and in the medicine cupboard? Write to the manufacturers of a range of products and ask for a list of ingredients. Once you receive the list, find out more about the chemicals used and their alternatives. You could follow this up by writing a letter to the manufacturers asking them if they have considered using less toxic ingredients. This can make a good research project, particularly for anyone interested in science or chemistry. There is a huge amount of information available on most chemicals used in household products, and many manufacturers have information on their own research.

Alternatives to household chemicals

Air fresheners

Try using scented plants such as lemon-scented geranium, rose leaves or lavender. Vinegar placed in an open dish is also effective.

Drain cleaner

Use a plunger or pour boiling water down the drain. Regular maintenance and not disposing of organic matter or hair down drains helps to prevent them become smelly or blocked.

Furniture polish

Use 1 tsp lemon oil in 0.5 litre mineral oil, or rub crushed, raw nuts on the wood for an oily polish.

Houseplant insecticides

Wash the leaves of your plant with soapy water, then rinse. You can also make an effective insecticide from washing-up liquid. Mix one teaspoonful of liquid with 0.5 litre (one pint) of water, and spray lightly. This is very useful against whitefly, but you should not overdo it. If you can get hold of a leaf infected with *Encarsia formosa* (see page 71), hang it at the side of the infected plant. Within a couple of days the whitefly scale will turn black.

Oven cleaner

Salt, baking soda, water—and elbow grease!

Silver cleaner

Soak silver in 1 litre warm water containing 1 tsp baking soda, 1 tsp salt and a piece of aluminium foil.

Window cleaner

Mix 2 tablespoons of vinegar in 1 litre of water. Apply with a clean cloth or leather. This old-fashioned method works surprisingly well.

Make your own cosmetics

Cosmetics and perfumes have been made at home for time out of mind. Perhaps the best known example is the use of rose petals and lavender for perfume, although I am sure that you can think of other natural perfumes and cosmetics. Lavender bags are easy to make using the flowers of lavender stitched up in a small bag. I remember, as a small child, a girl at school giving me one of these perfumed items. Several years later I found it in a drawer and it still retained its smell. Some people have qualms about using food products for cosmetics, but for most these soon disappear once they find out what commercial cosmetics are made of. There are several books you can get on making natural cosmetics and perfume, including *Natural Beauty* by R. Genders. However, here are a few ideas to have fun with in the meantime.

Moisturisers

Avocado moisturiser

A good moisturiser can be made by mixing the flesh of one avocado with a teaspoon of honey, a teaspoon of lemon juice and a natural yoghurt. Mix the ingredients until you have a stiff cream. Cool for 30 minutes or so, then massage the face with the resulting cream until it disappears. Leave overnight.

Egg yolk moisturiser

Egg yolks contain natural oils which will benefit normal skins. This one might leave you with egg on your face but it really works. Separate an egg yolk from the white and mix with a teaspoonful of almond oil and a teaspoonful of honey. Work the resulting cream into your skin with cotton wool and leave for around 30 minutes. Then wash off with warm water followed by cold water.

Cucumber moisturiser

A small cucumber mixed together with equal quantities of yoghurt and cream helps to smooth the skin and makes a good moisturiser. Cucumbers have remarkable properties—slices can also be used to help brighten your eyes.

136

Aftershave and perfume

The most common scent for men is aftershave, which is really very similar to female perfume. There are masses of different natural ingredients that can be used for perfume. The following recipe is good for aftershave.

Coriander aftershave

Take 65 grams (2¼ oz) of coriander seed—the older the seeds, the better the resulting aftershave—and mix with half a litre (one pint) of water and a tablespoon of honey. Simmer for 20 minutes. Cool and add one tablespoon of witch hazel. Strain into bottles and keep cool. Try out the result with some friends and see if they can guess what it is made of.

Hand lotion

Elderflower is a useful hand lotion, although you can experiment with other perfumed flowers using the technique described here. Take four to five handfuls of elderflowers and mix with a pot of petroleum jelly which has been warmed until melted. Leave for 40 minutes, reheating it once or twice as it cools. Sieve out the flowers and store the resulting cream in its original container. You can relabel it to make it more attractive.

Face packs

Here is a recipe that uses squashed tomatoes to give you a beautiful face. Boil a bowl of oatmeal for 20 minutes until you have a smooth paste. Sieve two or three ripe tomatoes into a bowl and mix in a small pot of natural yoghurt. Thoroughly mix the oatmeal with the other ingredients and cool. Protect your eyes and then apply the resulting cream thickly on your face. Leave for 30 minutes and then rinse off with cool water. If you repeat this treatment every month or so, it will keep your face looking fantastic.

If you enjoy experimenting with making your own cosmetics, I strongly recommend that you buy a book and find out more. Not only is this activity fun, but you also know that your cosmetic is made from natural ingredients and not tested on animals.

Goods survey

There are many ideas for environmental surveys of goods. You could, for instance, perform a packaging audit. From a week's shopping, make a note of every item of packaging and see if any is unnecessary. Could you have taken a container into the store to be refilled from a bulk container (many stores do not provide such facilities, but they could)? Which of the items are recyclable? Make a note of the three most overpackaged items and write to the manufacturers, asking what their policy on packaging is and pointing out that you consider the item to be overpackaged. Ask them if they have an environmental policy.

Another idea is to conduct a survey in a number of different stationery stores to see how many products they supply containing recycled material—it is a good idea to involve the store owner before you carry out survey work of this type. If you approach shop owners and tell them that you are doing the work as a part of an environmental project, most will be very reasonable. See if you can arrange an interview with the store owner, and ask if he or she has an environmental policy. If you discover very few recycled products, ask why more products made from recycled paper are not on sale.

Design a T-shirt

If you are a part of a group and would like to have something distinctive to take along to stalls or events, why not design and make your own T-shirt? A number of traders will produce T-shirts made to custom designs, which you can sell to recoup the cost of the exercise. Hold a competition among your friends to see who can come up with the best design. You should produce

138

the initial design as a piece of artwork, then get someone impartial to judge the results of your efforts. Go for a design that uses only one or two colours, as the T-shirt will then be cheaper to produce. Try to use unbleached cotton for the final product.

Where next? Spreading the word

Although many people are aware of the environmental crisis that the planet faces, many of them feel powerless to do anything about it, or do not know what to do beyond buying 'green' goods in the shop. Several recent market surveys among young people revealed that many regard purchasing green goods as the main action they can take in protecting the environment. It is making people more aware of the simple practical measures they could take that can help, more than anything, to bring about change. Ideally local, national and international initiatives should parallel each other. However, if there seems not to be much progress in your locality, why wait for national legislation when there is so much you can do yourselves right now? By the twin weapons of encouraging or starting local initiatives and lobbying for national and international change, young people can join in the process of improving the environment.

Write a teaching pack on the environment

If you are still at school or college you could get together with some friends and produce a teaching pack on environmental issues for younger children. You can make a good pack out of the issues surrounding green con-sumerism—there are very few about on the subject. If you are interested in writing, publishing and design, this is a fascinating activity. In order to carry out this activity well you should get together with one of your teachers or lecturers. If you know a teacher of younger children, you could even get your teaching pack tested in the classroom.

Choose an issue which you feel confident to write about, and on which you have loads of facts and figures. Decide on the target age group, bearing in mind that the language level should be suitable for the age you choose. In order to understand the language requirements of young children, look through a number of books written for your target age range.

Set out the aims of your pack. You might, for example, want children:

* to become more aware of recycling issues.
* to learn the difference between recycling and reuse.
* to understand that some materials are biodegradable while others, such as plastics, persist in the environment.

139

✿ to become aware of the role of governments and local authorities in the disposal and recycling of waste.

✿ to find out what they can do to help in the effort to recycle.

Decide which areas of the curriculum you would like to cover. It is worth bearing in mind that environmental issues can be incorporated in one way or another into nearly all areas of the curriculum. If you decide to make your pack cross-curricular, then you will have to decide for each worksheet which area of the curriculum should be covered.

For each of the learning objectives you have outlined for your pack you will need to put together a fact sheet and some classroom activities. If you decided to cover science, you would certainly need to include some good science experiments. On the issue of recycling, you may decide to examine biodegradability by burying a number of everyday items in the soil for a period of time. For each of these activities you would need to come up with step-by-step instructions describing how children should go about doing the task concerned, and include a list of necessary apparatus at the start of the sheet. It is also important to keep in mind safety factors.

I would suggest that no one person write the pack. The writing should be a team effort following discussion of the ideas. Use members of your peer group to give comments on the suitability of the text, and ask a teacher to make comments on the overall content and style of the pack. If a section you have written gets criticised, do not take it personally—this is an important part of the learning process for any writer.

Once your pack is finished, try to get it tested out on some children of your target age range. This type of exercise has been carried out successfully in several schools. The key to success is discussion and focusing accurately on the area of the curriculum you wish to cover.

9　Joining in

One of the biggest problems facing environmentalists has always been translating concern into action. Today, although many governments have begun to introduce new environmental legislation, progress often proceeds only at a snail's pace. In his State of the Union address of 1994, President Clinton referred to the environment no less than four times, twice in reference to proposed new legislation. At least that represents definite progress, even though many environmentalists still feel that current measures are only scratching the surface.

I hope that you have discovered by reading this book that there is a huge number of practical ways in which you can become involved. Local initiatives are valuable, and when multiplied throughout the world they have the power to make a considerable difference. However, local efforts need to be paralleled by national change, and these in turn by international change. That is why the United Nations Conference on Environment and Development, known as the Earth Summit, held at Rio de Janeiro in June 1992, was so important. The Earth Summit had implications for everyone, and its conclusions are essential reading for anyone starting out a campaign, because it details some of the measures that our governments have signed up to bring about.

THE EARTH SUMMIT

If you don't really want to read about some boring intergovernmental environment conference, I can't say that I would blame you. But the Earth Summit was no ordinary conference, and it was rarely boring. It marked a watershed in environmental history. Countries from all over the world got

141

around the table to discuss environmental issues and to set a common agenda to protect the environment. Coming 20 years after the UN conference on the human environment of June 1972, it also provided an opportunity for reflection. Then, the rich nations of the world had had to face up to some of the problems brought about by inequity between north and south. The question at Rio was how much had things changed in the intervening years?

The document that came out of the Rio summit was called *Agenda 21*. As a document, *Agenda 21* is not fun reading—not to put too fine a point on it, it is pretty turgid stuff. But if you can be bothered to wade through all the official prevarications, qualifications and issue-avoidance mechanisms, the document contains some really radical suggestions. For the first time ever it sets out measures to protect the environment on a global basis. It also has a whole chapter dedicated to young people, which commits governments to consulting young people on environmental issues. It recognises the right of young people to have a voice in decisions that affect their future, making it unique in terms of international initiatives, and giving young people a way to get involved in the political process and make their presence felt.

Unfortunately the young people at the Rio Summit itself ended up more or less gagged. Originally they were promised a whole hour of conference time, but the officials, perhaps in their enthusiasm to make the conference look non-confrontational and twee, decided to reduce this to ten minutes— or perhaps they were really running behind schedule. In the event, the cameras were turned off after only 120 seconds, and the world's reporters could not hear or see what was going on. What did go on? Well, the kids gave some of the delegates a hard time—they said things such as Third World debt should be written off, because rich countries had earned enough during the colonial period. This might be tough, true—but if you give young people a voice you have to be prepared to listen to what they have to say. After that the young people tried to hold a press conference and many were immediately arrested. People were shouted down and the whole thing looked very sad: so much for giving young people a voice. One or two delegates did speak up for young people and gave some of their views an airing, including US vice president Al Gore, a senator at the time. Apart from young people, the Earth Summit singled out two other groups for consultation and consideration in the policy-making process: women and native peoples. This was quite a breakthrough, bearing in mind that the concerns of these groups have rarely been taken into account.

What was discussed at Rio?

Agenda 21 is divided into 40 chapters, covering an enormous range of topics. It gives governments a green light to legislate on a whole number of issues from the air we breathe to biodiversity; the rights of women, children and indigenous peoples; social and economic cooperation and education; combating poverty; toxic chemicals and water quality; sustainable agriculture and much more. Each chapter gives governments a set of objectives setting out a way forward. The chapter on biodiversity, for example, recommends, among other things, that governments:

- develop national strategies for conservation.
- develop strategies for the conservation and sustainable use of biological resources.
- take measures to ensure the fair and equitable sharing of benefits derived from research.
- recognise and foster traditional methods and the knowledge of indigenous peoples.

The youth chapter states the following objectives, which I have quoted in full because it is important that you should know what they are.

25.4. Each country should, in consultation with its youth communities, establish a process to promote dialogue between the youth community and Government at all levels and to establish mechanisms that permit youth access to information and provide them with the opportunity to present their perspectives on government decisions, including the implementation of Agenda 21.

25.5. Each country, by the year 2000, should ensure that more than 50 per cent of its youth, gender balanced, are enrolled in or have access to appropriate secondary education or equivalent educational or vocational training programmes by increasing participation and access rates on an annual basis.

25.6. Each country should undertake initiatives aimed at reducing current levels of youth unemployment, particularly where they are disproportionately high in comparison to the overall unemployment rate.

25.7. Each country and the United Nations should support the promotion and creation of mechanisms to involve youth representation in all United Nations processes in order to influence those processes.

25.8. Each country should combat human rights abuses against young people, particularly young women and girls, and should consider providing all youth with legal protection, skills, opportunities and the support

143

necessary for them to fulfil their personal, economic and social aspirations and potentials.

To help ensure that some of these things actually happen in your country, you can find out about what is going on from the UN Information Centres (UNICs) in most capital cities. Alternatively you could contact Peace Child International at the Centre for Our Common Future, 52 rue de Parquis, 1201, Geneva, Switzerland.

BRINGING ABOUT NATIONAL AND INTERNATIONAL CHANGE

If you would like to join in with the efforts to bring about political change, there are many things that you can do, including joining a national environmental group, starting your own group or writing letters. There are a few important rules of thumb to make your work as effective as possible. Get your facts straight, don't go on hearsay. If something is your opinion, say so, because other people will have different opinions. Well-constructed arguments are based on substantiated knowledge. Be clear in what you say. It is often best to break arguments down into simple, bulleted lists. Express yourself using short, clear sentences. Be specific: the more you can hone an argument down to specifics, the better your chances of getting a message across. Unless you tell people specifically what they can do, the normal response tends to be, 'It's got nothing to do with me. What can I do about it?'

Environmental groups

Everybody can make a difference in protecting the environment, but getting together with others is fun and means that you can do even more. There are many ways in which you can join groups or even start your own. At the end of the book are names and addresses of groups covering almost every aspect of the environment: many have concessionary membership rates for young people; some are even free, or are affiliated to universities or colleges so that students can join without having to pay fees.

Volunteering

During your summer holidays you could consider volunteering for a group dealing with environment or development. Most groups require volunteers in order simply to keep going. Some camps and groups are involved specifically in practical conservation work. Many of the national groups involved

144

in this type of work are listed later, but there is also an enormous number of local groups involved in practical conservation, and these small groups are often more in need of volunteers than the large national organisations. One note of caution on volunteering: if you do decide to volunteer you have to be prepared to do whatever work is necessary to help the group concerned, and sometimes this is simple work such as photocopying or opening letters. This can come as a shock to volunteers who expect to start right away on practical hands-on initiatives. But it is sometimes the jobs that are least attractive that groups need doing the most. So you must be a bit philosophical about the type of work you are given, and be prepared to do whatever is necessary to help the group.

ACTIVITIES FOR ACTION

Many young people often feel that they can do little to stop the destruction of our environment. I hope that in this book I have shown that in fact there are many things the individual can do.

Campaigns

Bringing political change is difficult, but not impossible. Young people are at no particular disadvantage here, but making a difference politically is inevitably a slow and laborious process. What perhaps annoys many people the most about it is that heads of government and industry are daily willing to pay lip service to the environment and inflate their own often meagre political contributions. It would be more honest for such people to admit that there are many problems to overcome and open up the debate so that everyone could help find a way forward. One of the most powerful weapons in the environmental arsenal is government legislation, through which businesses can be made to conform to agreed standards, public transport systems can be encouraged and precious natural habitats can be protected. However, governments rarely act unless under pressure, so popular opinion is important in bringing about change, which is where campaigns come in.

By raising awareness of a particular issue, campaigns can help to rally public opinion. It often proves the case that, once a campaign has become successful, governments seek the advice of the pressure group running it. Even if a campaign is not entirely successful, the fact that a particular issue is being debated keeps that issue in the public eye, so that gradually awareness is raised. Young people can be just as successful at running a campaign as their elders. So if you feel strongly about a particular issue, why not start a campaign of your own? Bear in mind a few simple guidelines:

145

❧ Set goals—you can't change the world in one go.

❧ Decide on a strategy which focuses first on a particular aspect of the issue you are involved in.

❧ By publicising your initiative you can gain public interest, raise your chances of getting sponsorship, and encourage other similar initiatives. Publicity can take many different forms. You could consider giving a talk to your class or school assembly, producing a publicity leaflet, or producing a press release. The most effective forms of publicity are often those designed to grab the attention of a particular audience.

Writing letters—going to the top

Writing letters is the only way most people have of getting issues aired, and it is a surprisingly easy and effective way to bring concerns to the attention of local and national politicians. Many local and national government departments have a policy of answering all letters, but often the responses are very general and end up telling you nothing. Even if this is the case, writing letters is still worthwhile, because many politicians judge the importance of an issue by the amount of the mail they receive about it. Also, you may have an idea that a politician has never even thought of. Although writing a protest letter might not be your idea of a fun night, the efforts can prove well worthwhile. Sometimes you can help bring about change just simply by putting forward a good suggestion.

The knack of writing a good letter is to concentrate on a very specific issue. If you choose to write on a broad range of issues, the most likely response is a standard letter setting out current government policy. Very specific questions make people think and may even get all the way through to the politician. If you show that you are knowledgeable about current legislation you are less likely to get fobbed off. Use the government's own jargon terms and refer to their own statistics. This will pre-empt any attempt on their part to say, 'We are doing something about that already.'

Sending out a press release

Press releases are easy to put together and can be very effective: the local media will often give coverage to initiatives run by young people. There are a few general rules of thumb for preparing the material you send out.

Decide exactly what your story is, and try to use an angle that captures interest. For example, the launch of a recycling scheme by a group of young people constitutes a good story. Draft your release and if possible show it to someone who has experience of working with the press; otherwise, get someone to look through it and edit it for any grammatical, structural or spelling errors.

Check your facts. Do not let personal preferences influence what you say. Putting out false information is not only unethical—it may be libellous. Recently the fast-food chain McDonald's took two environmentalists to court for incorrectly stating that the company was responsible for rainforest destruction, among other things. In fact, McDonald's are very careful about checking the sources of their beef, and no beef for McDonald's burgers comes from land previously covered by rainforest. Think twice before starting campaigns against individual companies unless you know exactly what you are doing, are 100 per cent sure of the facts, and have clear, scientifically gathered evidence to justify your claims.

Write your release in clear, simple, unpretentious language. Aim for sentences of no more than 40 words. Break the text up into bullet points if you wish to make a series of related points. Put any additional or technical explanations in a section at the end of your release, called 'Editor's notes'.

If a picture or photo opportunity is available, make certain that you mention this in your release. Many press releases fail because a good photo opportunity has been missed. If you want to publicise an event, think of a good or interesting picture that can be organised. Many events get coverage on the strength of the photo opportunities alone. I remember recently a company anniversary which achieved national coverage because the company decided to fry the world's largest-ever pancake. You might decide against manufacturing the world's largest glass bottle to open a glass-recycling scheme, but an enormous bottle made of waste material might be a good idea. Go for something a little out of the ordinary.

Put the name of the group clearly at the top of your release, together with a return telephone/fax number. Make certain that it is absolutely clear who is making the release. Make sure that the press release contains one or two good quotes. It is perfectly all right to make them up, but make certain that the people concerned approve of what they are supposed to have said.

Sample Press releases

Pondsville College Recycling Campaign
10 June 1994

GOTTA LOTTA BOTTLE

Pondsville College Recycling Campaign announces a recycling centre launch at 1.00 p.m. on 1 July at Pondsville College.

A 30-foot bottle made out of used paper will be centre-stage at the launch of a new recycling scheme announced today by Pondsville College Recycling Campaign. The scheme is a district-wide initiative sponsored by Pondsville Council.

'We had great fun making the bottle,' said group leader Tony Cannit. 'Now, thanks to our initiative, the council will be placing bottle banks throughout the borough.'

Pondsville Mayor, Alex Chain, will be opening the first bottle bank at Pondsville College, in a special ceremony on 1 July at 1.00 p.m.

'The group has done a great job,' said Mr Chain. 'They have taken a positive lead, and I think that we can all learn a lot from them about how we can go about protecting the environment.'

The press are invited to a photocall at 12.30, when there will be an opportunity to photograph the group together with Mr Chain and the bottle.—For more information contact: Tony Cannit 0192-767-50302

Here is a sample press release taken from one issued from Greenpeace Canada. The release focuses on the campaign to protect the Great Lakes. You will notice how it refers very precisely to current international agreements and legislation. It also focuses on a single issue—that of the discharge of chlorine-based chemicals. A precise approach is more likely to achieve results than a scatter-gun approach.

GREENPEACE PRESS RELEASE

Environment Groups Charge Governments Fail to Protect Human Health and Great Lakes

TORONTO, Canada 6 July, 1994 (GP) A coalition of environmental groups charged that a new federal-provincial Great Lakes agreement will not protect human health and the environment and falls far short of international obligations with the United States.

The Canada-Ontario Agreement on Great Lakes Water Quality, signed today by environment ministers Sheila Copps and Bud Wildman, sets inadequate targets for the protection of human and ecosystem health and fails to implement repeated recommendations to phase out chlorinated poisons.

'It's worse than too little, too late,' said John Jackson, president of the 200-member coalition Great Lakes United. 'This compendium of tired old ideas, failing government programs and backsliding clearly shows that these governments do not have the political will to stop the contamination of the Great Lakes ecosystem.'

The agreement also fails to put in place an effective strategy for phasing

148

out and preventing further exposure to thousands of persistent toxins, including the class of chlorine-based poisons which the International Joint Commission (IJC) has recommended for elimination since 1992.

'Chlorine pollution is a major cause of preventable disease,' said Jay Palter of Greenpeace. 'The government's failure to agree to effective measures to prevent the use and discharge of thousands of chlorine-based poisons and other persistent toxins worsens their harmful effects on human health and the environment.'

The federal-provincial agreement establishes a 'phase-out' list of a mere handful of toxic substances and a 'voluntary' list of several more toxic substances.

'Over half of the toxic chemicals listed in the agreement for phase-out are already either banned, restricted or no longer used,' said Sarah Miller of the Canadian Environmental Law Association. 'This is largely a smoke-and-mirrors exercise to give the impression that new initiatives are being taken.'

In addition, the Agreement falls short of government commitments and obligations to clean-up the environment and protect public health. For example:

❧ The targets for the protection of human and ecosystem health are inadequate and largely immeasurable;

❧ Only nine of the 17 priority polluted areas on the Canadian side of the Great Lakes will be funded for clean-up, despite the fact that all 17 communities have developed clean-up plans, and federal funding for clean-ups has not substantially increased since 1986;

❧ The targets for habitat conservation, protected areas and biodiversity fall far short of commitments made in international agreements such as the UN biodiversity Convention signed in 1992.

The Canada-Ontario Agreement on Great Lakes Water quality sets out the measures by which the Canadian federal government and the province of Ontario will fulfil commitments made by Canada and the United States under the Great Lakes Water Quality Agreement.

The coalition of environmental groups represents Canadian Environmental Law Association (CELA), Canadian Institute for Environmental Law and Policy (CIELAP), Great Lakes United (GLU), Greenpeace, Pollution Probe, Sierra Club, and Women's Network for Health and Environment (WNHE).

For further information, contact:
(Contact names and numbers given).

Produce your own campaign publicity leaflet

A campaign publicity leaflet should be short and sharp, and designed to capture attention quickly. Unless you are producing a leaflet to answer a specific request for information, your heading should concentrate on getting the reader to read more. Remember that many people only read the first four or five words of a leaflet before throwing it away, so if you don't grab attention straight away your good work goes to waste. There is a number of ways of capturing attention, but a good image and caption combined are difficult to beat. You may decide for example to produce a recycling leaflet with the caption 'Why Should You Worry About Recycling?' together with a picture of a huge bulldozer on top of a mountain of waste.

The best leaflets are based around an effective design. Before you begin, look at several samples of other leaflets from a range of sources such as pressure groups or tourist information offices. Decide on which style you like the best. Very crowded leaflets are often the least effective. Sometimes groups produce too much copy for a leaflet, with the result that there is no room left for illustrations. You should aim to produce your leaflet in one or two colours. Two colours on a white or beige background produce effective results and are far cheaper to produce than full-colour leaflets. You will need to bear in mind the constraints imposed by your choice of colour before you begin. Many colour photos do not reproduce properly in black and white. Also, remember, if you want something that can be photocopied, that certain colours, such as light green, do not photocopy well.

The first stage is to design a mock-up version of your leaflet.

1 Take a piece of A4 paper and fold it into three, fan fashion. This will theoretically give you room for six sides of text.
2 Decide on any pictures or illustrations that you are going to use in your leaflet.
3 Design a front cover. You may decide to use a photo or an illustration of your own, in which case use a photocopy for this exercise. Above this you will eventually place the heading for your leaflet, so remember to leave a space. You should pencil this in for your mock-up version.
4 Open up your leaflet and try out several different arrangements of your illustrations until you are happy with the result, and then fix them lightly in place with some adhesive tape.
5 If you are happy with the result, you can now work out approximately how much text you will need to write for each column. A word length of around 50 to 100 words per column is often enough—although it is possible to fit in up to double this, the result is often too text heavy.

6 Once you have finalised the layout of your leaflet and written the text, you can use a standard desktop publishing package such as Pagemaker or Quark Express to produce the finished item; you can even use a good word-processor package such as Microsoft Word for Windows. Many colleges and schools have these packages available for students. Use a large type size for any headings. Leave frames where the graphics are to be inserted. You can experiment to get the best results.

7 Mark clearly on each graphic frame which picture you wish to have inserted. Make certain that the pictures are marked on the back too.

Once you have finished your leaflet you can print it. You may have a large enough budget to take the leaflet to a professional printer, and if you have decided to produce a two-colour leaflet you will need to be very clear about the colour arrangement. Otherwise you can run off your leaflet on a photocopier, in which case you should probably avoid using photographs as illustrations.

Organising your group

One of the most common problems faced by small groups is that one or two people end up doing all the work. The result of this is normally that peripheral members of the group become complacent and start relying on those taking the lead to do even more. When one of these central people decides he or she has done enough, the group folds.

The best way to avoid this problem is to anticipate it before it happens. Use effective delegation to involve all members of your group, and set clear deadlines so that people can plan their contribution. It is good that one or two people should lead the group, but they should not end up taking over the whole operation.

Make sure of people's skills and abilities. For example, if you have a group member who has a particular flair for design, get her to produce the publicity leaflet for your group. This might sound obvious, but it is something that often does not happen. Don't allow your prejudices to rule your decisions: many people need space and time to show their abilities. Give people a chance but be clear with them if their work has not been up to scratch—avoid confrontations, except in the last resort.

Have fun. People will work a lot harder if they are enjoying themselves. If some of your activities are a bit drab, have a meeting and think of some ways of livening things up. I have heard of groups having discussions and role plays or listening to music at the same time as stuffing envelopes. Envelope-stuffing is deadly boring. If you are involved in an activity such as this make certain that no one person carries the whole can, and try to think of some distraction to keep people smiling. Try to keep everyone involved and avoid cliques developing. If you are having a discussion, make certain that everyone has a chance to speak.

The legal side of running a group

Although laws vary from country to country, there are some pretty general guidelines to ensure that your group does not accidentally engage in anything illegal.

* Make certain that you don't put out any information that slanders any individual or company, as in the McDonald's case. Check your facts—remember that facts and figures given in published information are not always reliable. This may not be the fault of the author: what is true one year may not be true the next. But misinformation is sometimes perpetuated by successive authors. Facts and figures can be incredibly difficult to check—if in doubt, leave it out.
* Do not refer even indirectly to any legal case currently being tried in the courts.
* If your group is involved in any protests or direct action, make certain that they are within the law. Avoid trouble at all costs. I would advise the greatest caution before taking part in any activity of this kind. For many groups, lobbying, practical programmes and publicity

152

programmes prove just as effective as direct action—which can sometimes result in negative publicity.

If you are involved in organising any sponsored events involving a large number of people, let the police and town authorities know well in advance.

Make safety your first consideration on all occasions.

If your group has funds, make certain that you keep a set of books in which all costs and expenditures are detailed. Appoint a treasurer and get someone to audit the books once a year to make certain that no mistakes have been made.

These guidelines should help you avoid falling foul of the law. Above all, remember the golden rule—if you think that something might be illegal, check before you do it.

Computer networks

Using computer networks is a convenient and cheap way of keeping up to date with environmental initiatives throughout the world. Increasing numbers of initiatives involving young people are available over the networks. Many environmentalists now use the Internet for communication, and it is a great way of keeping in touch with people who think in the same way as yourself. One recently established initiative is the EarthWeb project (see back of book for address), which aims to provide a vital new hypertext-based link between individuals interested in the environment with databases, statistics, projects and environmental information from all around the world. My own email address is jhowson @ gn.apc.org.

Further Information

One of the best ways of becoming involved in collective action to protect the environment is to join one of the many organisations available throughout the world. The following list is by no means complete, but I have tried to cover many of the organisations campaigning on issues covered by this book.

ORGANISATIONS IN THE UK

Animal Aid

7 Castle Street, Tonbridge, Kent TN7 IBH.
Campaigns on animal rights issues and factory farming.

The Born Free Foundation

Cherry Tree Cottage, Coldharbour, Dorking, Surrey RH5 6HA.

British Trust for Conservation Volunteers

36 St Mary's Street, Wallingford, Oxfordshire OX10 0EU.
Tel: 01491–39766
Works on a range of excellent practical conservation projects for people of all ages.

The Centre for Alternative Technology

The Quarry, Machynlleth, Powys, Wales SY20 9AZ.
The Centre for Alternative Technology promotes the sustainable use of energy. The site uses and displays a wide range of renewable energy resources, energy efficient buildings and technologies which can be viewed by the public. Holiday cabins are available for young people wishing to experience the sustainable use of energy at first hand.

Centre for Sustainable Energy
incorporating **Bristol Energy Centre**

CREATE Centre, B-Bond Warehouse, Smeaton Road, Bristol BS1 6XN.
The Centre carries out a range of activities which include: practical insulation and energy advice work for low income families, elderly and disabled people; training and examining in energy awareness; environmental education and a variety of commercial, energy-saving work.

Council for Environmental Education (CEE)

University of Reading, London Road, Reading, Berkshire RG1 5AQ.
National organisation promoting environmental education for England and Wales (Scotland has its own organisation). CEE produces a newsletter for schools as well as bibliographies, and details of environmental education resources.

Department of the Environment

Romney House, 43 Marsham Street, London SW1P 3EB.
Tel: 0171 276 0900
The DoE produces reports and information leaflets, and also awards grants to small environmental organisations.

Friends of the Earth

26–28 Underwood Street, London N1 7JQ.
Tel: 0171 490 1555
Fax: 0171 490 0881
Friends of the Earth is a campaigning pressure group. It concentrates on putting pressure on governments and decision-makers on a wide range of environmental issues, including air pollution, water pollution, forestry and energy use. Friends of the Earth is an international organisation with affiliated groups in more than 50 different countries. In the UK it has a network of around 300 local groups and an education programme. Some Friends of the Earth affiliated groups have programmes targeted at schools and young people.

155

Friends of the Earth Scotland

Bonnington Mill, 70–72 Newhaven Road, Edinburgh EH6 5QG.
An independent Friends of the Earth group working on Scottish environmental issues.

GreenNet

393–395 City Road, 4th Floor, London EC1V 1NE.
email: Support @ gn.apc.org
A computer network committed to environment and development. It is a small voluntary organisation with amazingly reasonable prices. GreenNet links into the internet through the Association for Progressive Communications. There are many conferences for students and access to university computers around the world. If you are a computer nut and not already a member, join.

Greenpeace

Canonbury Villas, London N1 2HB.
Tel: 0171–354 5100.
An international pressure group whose members take part in many high-profile direct actions to protect the environment, but also carry out lobbying work. They campaign on a wide range of issues including water pollution, air pollution, whales and dolphins, and nuclear issues.

International Institute for Environmental Development (IIED)

3 Endsleigh Street, London WC1H ODD.
Tel: 0171–388 2117
Fax: 0171–388 2826
Works on a range of issues concerned with promoting sustainable development.

National Association for Environmental Education (UK)

University of Wolverhampton, Walsall Campus, Gorway, Walsall WS1 3BD.
Tel: 01922 31200

National Society for Clean Air

136 North Street, Brighton, Bristol BS4 3JP.

Oxfam

274 Banbury Road, Oxford OX2 7DZ.
Major international organisation working on development issues and famine relief. Produces first class information.

Population Concern

231 Tottenham Court Road, London W1P 9AE.
Tel: 0171 631 1546
Fax: 0171 436 2143
An organisation working on population issues, involved in fund-raising for population and development programmes worldwide.

Royal Society for the Protection of Birds (RSPB)

The Lodge, Sandy, Bedfordshire SG19 2DL.
The RSPB is Britain's largest charity dealing with environmental issues. Although it specialises in work to protect birds, it has also been involved in work on threatened habitats. The RSPB has an education programme to involve teachers in conservation issues and a club for young people, the YOC (Young Ornithologists Club).

Survival International

310 Edgware Road, London W2 1DY.
Tel: 0171 723 5535
An international organisation that works for the rights of threatened tribal peoples and brings their plight to public attention.

Tidy Britain

The Pier, Wigan WN3 4EX.
Although Tidy Britain focuses primarily on litter issues including cleaner beaches, it also promotes recycling and the sustainable use of resources. The organisation boasts a first class education department.

Transport 2000

Walkden House, 10 Melton Street, London NW1 2EJ.
Tel: 0171 388 8386
Transport 2000 is a national pressure group specialising in transport and road issues and promoting a more sustainable transport system.

Vegetarian Society

Parkdale, Dunham Road, Altrincham, Cheshire WA14 4QG.
Deals with a range of issues related to vegetarianism and diet. It produces among other things a good teaching pack, which contains a wealth of detailed material on food issues.

The Wildlife Trust

The Green, Witham Park, Lincoln LN5 7JR.
The Wildlife Trust has a section for young people (9–13) known as Wildlife Watch. Wildlife Watch concentrates on practical projects to monitor pollution, raise awareness and bring about change.

Women's Environmental Network (WEN)

Aberdeen Studios, 22 Highbury Grove, London N5 2EA.
Tel: 0171 354 8823
A non-profit-making organisation educating and empowering women interested in environmental issues. WEN gives excellent information on a number of issues relating to women.

World Wide Fund for Nature (WWF)

Panda House, Wayside Park, Goldalming, Guildford, Surrey GU7 1XR.
An environmental pressure group specialising in the protection of wildlife and natural systems. The World Wide Fund provides excellent information as well as being involved in many good practical initiatives on the ground. As one of the world's largest groups of its kind, it plays a key role. The World Wide Fund has a first class education programme, which is engaged in work in many countries throughout the world.

WWF International

Av. du Mont-Blanc, 1196 Gland, Switzerland.

ORGANISATIONS IN THE UNITED STATES

The USA boasts more environmental organisations than any other country in the world. These campaign on almost every issue imaginable. Many produce useful information for young people. If you are writing for information, don't forget to send some money to cover the cost of your postage. If telephoning from outside the USA, dial 001 before the numbers given below.

Adopt a Stream Foundation

P.O. Box 5558, Everett, WA 98201.
Tel: (206) 388–3313

American Oceans Campaign

725 Arizona Avenue, Suite 102, Santa Monica, CA 90401.
Tel: (213) 576–6162

Carrying Capacity Network

1325 G Street NW, Suite 1003, Washington, DC 20005.
Tel: (202) 879–3045

The Centre for Economic Conversion

222 View Street, Mt. View, CA 94041–1344.
Tel: (415) 968–8798
Fax: (415) 968–1126

The Centre for Marine Conservation

1725 DeSales Street, NW, Suite 500, Washington, DC 20036.
Tel: (202) 429–5609

The Conservation Fund

1800 North Kent Street, Suite 1120, Arlington, VA 22209.
Tel: (703) 525–6300

159

The Cousteau Society

870 Greenbrier Circle, Suite 402, Chesapeake, VA 23320.
Tel: (804) 523–9335

EarthPhase Foundation

706 Frederick Street, Santa Cruz, CA 95063.
Deals with issues of food and vegetarianism, often from an environmental perspective.

The EarthWeb Project

204 Divide View Drive, Golden, CO 80403.
email: hinckley @ netcom.com

Environmental Defence Fund

257 Park Avenue South, New York, NY 10010.
Tel: (212) 505–2100

The Environmental Exchange

1718 Connecticut Ave. NW, Suite 600, Washington, DC 20009.
Tel: (202) 387–2182

Global Tomorrow Coalition

1325 G Street NW, Suite 915, Washington, DC 20005–3104.
Tel: (202) 628–4016

Global Releaf

P.O. Box 2000, Washington, DC 20013.
Tel: (202) 667–3300

Izaak Walton League of America

1401 Wilson Boulevard, Level B, Arlington, VA 22209–2318.
Tel: (703) 528–1818

Keep America Beautiful, Inc.

Mill River Plaza, 9 West Broad Street, Stamford, CT 06902.
Tel: (203) 323–8987

National Audubon Society

700 Broadway, New York, NY 10003.
Tel: (212) 979–3000

The National Geographic Society

1145 17th Street NW, Washington, DC 20036.
Tel: (202) 857–7000

The National Institute for Urban Wildlife

10921 Trotting Ridge Way, Columbia, MD 21044.
Tel: (301) 995–1119

National Parks and Conservation Association

1776 Massachusetts Avenue, Washington, DC 20036.
Tel: (202) 223–6722

National Toxics Campaign

29 Temple Place/5th Floor, Boston, MA 02111.
Tel: (617) 482–1477

National Wildlife Federation

1400 Sixteenth Street NW, Washington, DC 20036–2266.
Tel: (703) 790–6800

The Nature Conservancy

1815 North Lynn Street, Arlington, VA 22209.
Tel: (703) 841–5300

North American Association for Environmental Education (NAAEE)

1255 23rd Street NW, Washington, DC 20037.
Membership and Publications: P.O. Box 400, Troy, OH 45373.
Tel: (513) 676–2514
The NAAEE promotes environmental education in the USA.

Population-Environment Balance

1325 G Street NW, Suite 1003, Washington, DC 20005–3104.
Tel: (202) 879–3000

Project Eco-School

881 Alma Real Drive, Suite 300, Pacific Palisades, CA 90272.
Tel: (310) 454–4585

Renew America

1400 Sixteenth Street NW, Suite 710, Washington, DC 20036.
Tel: (202) 232–2252

The Sierra Club

730 Polk Street, San Francisco, CA 94109.
Tel: (415) 923–5660
The Sierra Club is one of the United States' best known environmental organisations. It works on a wide range of issues and produces many good publications.

Soil Conservation Society of America

7515 NE Ankeny Road, Ankeny, IA 50021.
Tel: (515) 289–2331

World Resources Institute

1709 New York Avenue NW, Washington, DC 20006.
Tel: (202) 662–3085

WorldWatch Institute

1776 Massachusetts Avenue NW, Washington, DC 20036.
Tel: (202) 452–1999
The WorldWatch Institute produces a wide range of high-quality information and research papers on environmental and development issues.

The World Wide Fund for Nature

1250 Twenty-Fourth Street NW, Washington, DC 20037.
Tel: (202) 293–4800

Zero Population Growth

1400 16th Street NW, Suite 320, Washington, DC 20036.
Tel: (202) 332–2200

ORGANISATIONS IN AUSTRALIA

Australian Conservation Foundation (ACF)

340 Gore Street, Fitzroy, Victoria 3065.

Friends of the Earth

PO Box A474, Sydney, New South Wales 2001.

Greenpeace Australia

National Office, PO Box 800, 41 Holt Street, Surrey Hills, New South Wales 2010.

ORGANISATIONS IN NEW ZEALAND

Friends of the Earth

PO Box 5599, Wellersley Street, Auckland West.

Greenpeace (New Zealand)

Private bag 92507, Wellersley Street, Auckland.

163

New Zealand Natural Heritage Foundation
Massey University, Parmerstone North.

ORGANISATIONS IN CANADA

Friends of the Earth
251 Laurier Avenue West, Suit 701, Ottawa, Ontario K1P 5JS.

Greenpeace Canada
6th Floor, 185 Spadina Avenue, Toronto, Ontario MST-2C6.

Further Reading

The 'Conserving our World' Series, Wayland (1989–91).
A very good series of books covering most environmental issues for 9 to 13-year-olds. Written in clear and understandable language.

Young Person's Action Guide to Animal Rights, Barbara James, Virago.
This book is one of the best I have seen on animal rights issues, it tells the story as it is, tells you what you can do to help, but doesn't aim to shock on every page.

Desertification, McLeish, Wayland.
A good introduction to this often neglected area, well written and interesting.

Friends of the Earth Education Sheets, Friends of the Earth UK.
This very informative series of sheets is well worth getting hold of, aimed at those completing projects at school but good for anyone with an interest in the environment.

Greenpeace Book of Dolphins, John May, Random Century Group.
A very good and authoritative introduction to dolphins and the threats they face.

Save the Earth, Jonathon Porritt (ed), Dorling Kindersley.
A good collection of articles from experts on a range of environmental issues.

In the Rainforest, Catherine Caufield, Picador, 1986.
A classic, although heavy going in places as it is written for an adult audience. Nevertheless this book is full of good background information and case studies.

Natural Beauty, R. Genders, Webb & Bower.
A thoroughly good read for anyone interested in beauty without cruelty.

The Green PC, Steve Anzovin, TAB Books, PO Box 40, Blue Ridge Summit, PA17294-0850, USA.
Full of tips and hints, not all of which you will find yourself agreeing with, but a good read and thought-provoking.

Rescue Mission Planet Earth: a children's edition of agenda 21. Children's Task Force for Agenda 21, Kingfisher Books.
A useful outline of the Earth Summit aimed at younger readers, very readable, good fun.

Young Green Consumer's Guide, Elkinton and Hales, Gollancz.
Still one of the best books around for finding out what is environmentally sound and what is not. Written in clear language and covering a range of issues.

The Green Consumer's Guide, Elkinton and Hales, Gollancz.
The adult version of the previous book. It contains far more detail on individual purchases than the younger version. Although becoming a little dated now, it is still a classic.

Considering Conservation and *Conservation 2000*, Batsford Books.
Two series of books by Philip Neal for secondary schools, with titles covering all the topics discussed in this book.

BOOKS FOR RESEARCH AND REFERENCE

The Recycling Officer's Handbook, Friends of the Earth.
Aimed at Local Government Officers, this book is a goldmine of facts and figures. Get your local library to obtain a copy as it is rather expensive and definitely not the type of book that you would want to read just for the fun of it.

Earth Summit 92, Joyce Quarrie, The Regency Press, 1992.
Although aimed at an adult audience and heavy reading, this book gives a good synopsis of Agenda 21. A book to borrow from the library rather than purchase.

Index

167

170